IN
SEARCH
OF THE
COMMON
GOOD

CHRISTIAN
FIDELITY
IN A
FRACTURED
WORLD

JAKE MEADOR

FOREWORD BY TIMOTHY KELLER

ivp

An imprint of InterVarsity Press
Downers Grove, Illinois

InterVarsity Press
P.O. Box 1400 | Downers Grove, IL 60515-1426
ivpress.com | email@ivpress.com

InterVarsity Press® is the publishing division of InterVarsity Christian Fellowship/USA®. For more information, visit intervarsity.org.

All Scripture quotations, unless otherwise indicated, are taken from The Holy Bible, New International Version®, NIV®. Copyright © 1973, 1978, 1984, 2011 by Biblica, Inc.™ Used by permission of Zondervan. All rights reserved worldwide. www.zondervan.com. The "NIV" and "New International Version" are trademarks registered in the United States Patent and Trademark Office by Biblica, Inc.™

While any stories in this book are true, some names and identifying information may have been changed to protect the privacy of individuals.

Excerpts from "The Dry Salvages" and "Little Gidding" are from *Four Quartets* by T. S. Eliot. Copyright © 1941, 1942 by T. S. Eliot, renewed 1969, 1970 by Esme Valerie Eliot. Reprinted by permission of Houghton Mifflin Harcourt Publishing Company. All rights reserved.

Published in association with the literary agent Don Gates of The Gates Group, www.the-gates-group.com.

Cover design: David Fassett
Interior design: Daniel van Loon
Images: © Arnaud Lecamus / 500px / Getty Images

ISBN 978-0-8308-4554-5 (hardcover) | ISBN 978-1-5140-1396-0 (paperback) |
ISBN 978-0-8308-7378-4 (digital)

Library of Congress Cataloging-in-Publication Data
Names: Meador, Jake, author.
Title: In search of the common good : Christian fidelity in a fractured world / Jake Meador.
Description: Downers Grove : InterVarsity Press, 2019. | Includes bibliographical references.
Identifiers: LCCN 2019007950 (print) | LCCN 2019012623 (ebook) | ISBN 9780830873784 (eBook) |
    ISBN 9780830845545 (hardcover : alk. paper)
Subjects: LCSH: Common good–Religious aspects–Christianity.
Classification: LCC BR115.P7 (ebook) | LCC BR115.P7 M36 2019 (print) | DDC 261.0973--dc23
LC record available at https://lccn.loc.gov/2019007950

TO MY WIFE, JOIE MEADOR

The Vanaukens said it best. If it's half as good as the half we've known, here's "hail!" to the rest of the road.

TO MY PARENTS, ROB AND RUTH MEADOR

You taught me courage, patience, and fidelity. You taught me to love what is good and hate what is evil. You taught me to fight for what is true, even when it hurts and even when it is costly.

TO DAVY JOY MEADOR

May you always be eager, sharp, and devoted to God.

TO ROBERT WENDELL MEADOR

May you always keep faith.

TO AUSTIN FRANCIS MEADOR

May you give yourself to good work.

These are only hints and guesses,
Hints followed by guesses; and the rest
Is prayer, observance, discipline, thought, and action.
The hint half guessed, the gift half understood, is Incarnation.

T. S. ELIOT, "THE DRY SALVAGES"

Christians should confess their faith in the natural order as the good creation
of God. To do this is to acknowledge that there are limits to the employment
of technique and limits to the appropriateness of our "making." These limits
will not be taught us by compassion, but only by the understanding of what
God has made, and by a discovery that it is complete, whole, and satisfying.

OLIVER O'DONOVAN, *BEGOTTEN OR MADE?*

I ask all of you, dear brothers and sisters, to view these things that are happening
in our historical moment with a spirit of hope, generosity, and sacrifice.... If we
illuminate with Christian hope our intense longings for justice and peace and
all that is good, then we can be sure that no one dies forever. If we have imbued
our work with a sense of great faith, love of God, and hope for humanity, then
all our endeavors will lead to the splendid crown that is the sure reward for the
work of sowing truth, justice, love, and goodness. Our work does not remain here;
it is gathered and purified by the Spirit of God and returned to us as a reward.

OSCAR ROMERO, *THE SCANDAL OF REDEMPTION*

(The) way of life out of and toward communion with God is achieved in the
world itself through which we know Him. Luther's idea that God is ever present
in masks and mummeries surrounding us on all sides rules out any attempt by
man to narrow down reality to manageable proportions; God is everywhere, and
vocation—calling—is arriving from every direction and in all sorts of ways.

PETER ESCALANTE, "PHILOSOPHY AS A WAY OF LIFE: REFORMING
THE QUEST FOR WISDOM"

CONTENTS

TIMOTHY KELLER

I HAVE BEEN AN ORDAINED MINISTER for nearly forty-five years. When I entered the ministry, most of the divisions in the church seemed to be doctrinal. There were controversies about the charismatic gifts and Pentecostalism, about the end times and the Second Coming of Christ, about predestination and free will, about the meaning of baptism and the Lord's Supper. I entered a Presbyterian denomination in which there was a high degree of consensus on all those issues. Yet today my church, like so many others, is sharply divided, despite the fact that its ministers can agree on a very long and detailed doctrinal statement, the Westminster standards.

So why all the conflict? It is not as much over doctrine as over what our relationship to the culture should be. And as I look around, I see this same division roiling Christian denominations and organizations everywhere.

When my adult lifetime began our society was one where most people felt some social pressure to attend church. It was also one in which much of historic Christian morality was assumed, respected, or at least understood. All that has changed. Today as younger Christian adults live out their lives—at work, in college classrooms and dorm rooms, in diversity training sessions at the office, online, or simply consuming the latest television series—they realize that they are considered to be extremists (particularly if they speak up).

Not only is mainstream culture moving farther away from Christian beliefs, but it also seems to be weakening and fragmenting. There is enormous dissatisfaction with the political establishments, and people are willing to vote for candidates both right and left that even ten years ago would have been considered too extreme. We have resurgent socialism as well as blood-and-soil populism. US life expectancy has dropped three years in a row—an unprecedented phenomenon outside of wartime. There is agreement that loneliness and isolation, suicide and addiction, are growing alarmingly as community and communities break down.

In this new situation, many of the older Christian models of "cultural engagement" or "political theology" seem obsolete. One was pietism, the view that believers should be about winning souls and building up the church, and not about trying to be Christians in "politics." But that approach assumes a well-functioning society that doesn't need Christians to support the common good. If society is breaking down, how can you love your neighbor without getting politically involved? And what if your culture comes to *define* your soul-winning as a politically illegitimate act? How do you avoid politics then?

Another Christian approach was that of the Religious Right. It focused on a number of policy issues tied to traditional Christian doctrines about how people should live, though it singled out only some—matters of abortion, marriage, and religious freedom. (It never spent time thinking out the implications of Christian teaching on matters of race, economics, or justice.) Then it sought through electoral politics to put people into power who promoted those chosen policies. There was great optimism and hope for this approach beginning in the mid-1970s and lasting almost thirty years. But both in the arena of law (e.g., the *Windsor* and *Obergefell* decisions) and that of public opinion we have seen an overwhelming wave of indifference or antipathy to historical Christian understandings of sex, gender, and marriage. This, tied to the now steep drop in religious affiliation and church attendance (at least 66 percent of all Christian churches are now in decline), spells a shrinking voter base for the Religious Right.

Younger Christians have turned away from these approaches led by those of my generation and are looking elsewhere. One option has been a kind of new monasticism that rightly promotes much stronger and "thicker" Christian community but also largely gives up on any hope of influencing the civic order. Other approaches, however, run the risk of getting caught up in the broader political polarization and becoming mere tools of it, just one part of a left or right political coalition. For example, we may see the development of both "blue evangelicalism" and "red evangelicalism" online. The former talks about racial and economic justice, but is quiet about the biblical teaching on subjects such as abortion, sexuality, and gender. The latter condemns sexual immorality and secularism in the strongest terms but grows silent when its political allies fan the flames of racial resentment toward immigrants. When the church, in the name of political power, allies and aligns too much with the current secular left or right, it is sapped of both spiritual power and credibility with nonbelievers. Theologically, both political poles are suspect, because one makes an idol out of individual freedom, and the other makes an idol out of race and nation, blood and soil. In both something created and earthly is deified. Extreme progressivism detaches individuals from community and history and any concept of virtue, but the nationalism and racism that might replace it are no answer to it.

If you are looking for a way forward, I can think of no better starting point than this book. There are many things I love about the volume in your hands, but above all I love how Jake Meador is so accessible as he lays out a path that avoids not only problems of the Christianity-and-culture models of my generation but also those of his. There is deep reading and learning behind this eminently readable essay.

In the first two parts of the book, Jake does a great job of summarizing and explaining the critique of late modern culture brought out by Charles Taylor and others. In parts three and four, he strikes the best balance I have seen between an emphasis on Christians building a counter-culture and on Christians being unique, good citizens in society.

And in Jake's telling these two things are not merely "two wings of a plane," but are integrally connected. Christians are unique citizens in society because, formed by the "upside-down" kingdom of God, they move out into the world as self-sacrificers rather than self-actualizers. Late modern secularism instills deep the notion that we should never give up our interests or rights for anyone else, we should always assert ourselves, and we should be righteously angry as we do so. That of course leads to the dog-eat-dog economy and society we have, all in the name of freedom. In Jake's compelling vision, Christian character, formed in a worshiping community, creates true "public servants." So Christian counter-culture produces (and Christian beliefs can form the basis for) civic virtue.

Chapter nine is particularly helpful to Christians seeking faithful political presence in a secular world. Here Jake clarifies the crucial difference between Christian doctrines, which are biblically rooted, and public policies, which are matters of prudence. He also takes "solidarity," "sphere sovereignty," and "subsidiarity," concepts from various branches of Reformed and Catholic thought, and shows how eminently practical each is for thinking out our political involvements as believers. Everywhere he avoids pietism and partisanship, withdrawal or co-option.

So read this book—and then discuss it with someone. Advance the conversation we must have if we are going to make real changes. There's no more urgent topic for the church in the West than this, and that is especially true for Protestants and evangelicals. *In Search of the Common Good* is an important contribution, and I'm glad to recommend it to you.

INTRODUCTION

Love is a circle that turns with no end. Life is a line under gravity's bend.

ERIC TONJES, "LIE WITH ME LOVER"

ON FEBRUARY 19, 1895, in Oakland, Nebraska, a twenty-nine-year-old Swedish immigrant and tenant farmer named Carl Gotfred Fredstrom tried to kill himself.

He failed.

The next day that same young man stood in the front of a church next to a woman named Elise Carlson, eight years his junior, and took his wedding vows. Their family began, quite literally, under the shadow of death—or attempted death, as it were.

Over 123 years later in a small hotel room fifty-seven miles down the road from where Carl (known to his friends as C. G.) and Elise married, a group of around thirty people gathered together to share a meal, to catch up, and to remember. Several of them told stories from their childhood of visiting their grandparents. They particularly remembered the way their grandpa loved to garden, loved to make iced tea, and how he would drink his coffee: he poured it from the pot into a mug and from the mug into a smaller cup that sat on a saucer—the multiple pours helped cool the coffee to a safe drinking temperature. He then slurped the coffee, making a noise that filled the whole room and drowned out all attempts at conversation. Grandpa had a large mustache and did not want the coffee to get into it.

They told these stories with smiles, laughter, and a fondness you could both see in their eyes and hear in their voices.

These people gathered together in Omaha in the summer of 2018 to celebrate a family reunion were C. G. and Elise's grandchildren.

Last year I saw a sign in Grand Central Station that asked, "Why do you love the world?" It was an ad from Lufthansa Airlines, and its whole purpose was to stir whatever love you feel in such a way that you would spend lots of money buying plane tickets from Lufthansa to see the world you (presumably) love.

Despite such questionable motivations, I couldn't help being struck by that question.

It isn't an unreasonable one. Christian writer Steven Garber has said that one of the greatest questions any of us will face is whether we can know the world and still love it.[1] And that question feels especially poignant in today's America.

The America of 2019 is a place in clear decline. We have had to create a new category—deaths of despair—to speak about the social crisis existing in much of our country, where deaths due to suicide, alcoholism, and drug overdoses are skyrocketing.[2] It is a place where racial minorities live with the daily fear of deportation, police violence, or worse. It is a place where many younger Americans report being unable to speak with their family about personal matters due to seemingly irresolvable divides that have opened up between them in the era of President Trump. It is a place where a man like Jeff Bezos can make millions of dollars in a couple of hours while other Americans do not even have access to clean water, and where in a single year over 650,000 human lives are ended before they can even begin.

Can you love a world like that? *Should* you love a world like that? And even if you can and should love the world, what good can that do if there isn't anything you hold in common with others that you all love together? Theologian Oliver O'Donovan says that healthy communities must be organized around what he calls "common objects of love."[3] But do we *have* any such objects in America today?

My friend Eric wrote a song in the midst of a personal tragedy wrestling with the nature of grief and loss. He said in it that "love is a circle that turns with no end / but life is a line under gravity's bend."[4] The line is itself an echo of Dante's closing lines in the *Divine Comedy*, where the great Italian poet wrote of "the Love which moves the sun and the other stars," likening it to "a wheel that equally is moved."[5] Dante believed that the deepest truth about the universe is that it is animated by love, that it is held together and made to turn by the love of God. And Dante was not being poetic—he believed that was actually how the universe worked.

This is a powerful picture of the world when we stop to think about it. In Dante's world, the most natural thing a person can do, the most normal thing, is to love. For, if Dante is right, then Love himself is what holds the world together. This is not mere sentiment, a repeating of pleasant-sounding ideas meant to make ourselves feel better. If Christianity is true, then this is actually how the world works—Love moves the sun and the other stars, it causes the sun to rise, rain to fall, and it sustains your life and mine.

But in a world groaning beneath the weight of evil and suffering, it can be hard to believe such a thing. We do not see the circle turning, but we do feel the fragile line of our life—or the lives of those we love— bending beneath the weight of gravity.

This book presupposes that even in a world like ours, Dante is still right. The force that holds the cosmos together is both a personal being and is purely, perfectly love. And if that is true, then we can ask questions not only about the universe but also about ourselves, about the nature of the good life, and about work and membership. And we can answer those questions in ways that agree with the natural love that animates the world. As we live in this world, we can discern within it something deeper, something that speaks to the hidden longings of our hearts and tells us that those desires will one day find satisfaction.

Gravity presses down on us. Indeed, if we are to try to create a world that more closely reflects the essential truth about creation—that love binds the world together—then we must understand the things threatening that love. And as we consider the Christian story, we will realize that only the things that are broken and die, the things pressed down and crushed by gravity, can be resurrected. Because that is true, we can actually have real hope for our life together in the world, and we can even understand what that life ought to be.

Gravity presses down on us, and sometimes it seems to overwhelm us entirely. On that cold February night in 1895, it nearly did. But if Christianity is true, gravity does not have the final word. Love does. So 123 years later, a number of C. G. and Elise's grandchildren gathered together to remember. Now, 124 years later, you are reading a book written by C. G. and Elise's great-grandson.

The same stars that turned round the world in 1895, that looked down on C. G. as he considered ending his life, spin today. And they are still propelled by the love that called the world into being. But we can say something more. Love called the world into being, yes. It also calls to us today. It invites us into a life that would subvert the crushing power of sin and death, a life that proves the truth spoken of in St. John's Apocalypse: "Behold, I make all things new." We are made new by love, yes. But so is the world. And in that there is hope.

PART ONE

THE

BREAKDOWN

OF

COMMUNITY

IT'S BEEN SIXTY YEARS since W. H. Auden wrote his lengthy poem "The Age of Anxiety." In the time since we have, if anything, become more anxious than ever. Christians worry over the continued life of their religious communities and institutions. In the political sphere, both left and right look to the future with concern, struggling to identify a sure path toward flourishing. Neither side can agree on the goods they wish to pursue together, so that the triumphs of the right appear as catastrophic defeats for the left, and vice versa. In such a society, it is very hard to discern any sort of common good that can unify us. Later in this book, we'll talk about what needs to be done. But we need to begin by defining the problem as it exists today.

First, we must face the fact that many of the wounds contributing to the American church's decline are self-inflicted. Though American Christians do have genuine opponents in the public square and in elite institutions, they have often been their own worst enemies, making disastrous political compromises and looking the other way when sin is exposed in their midst—when addressing that sin would require sacrifices they have deemed too costly, or risks deemed too dangerous. A conservative columnist once used the phrase "decline is a choice" when describing American foreign policy. Something similar applies to the decline of the American church. Our decline is a predictable product of choices we have made. If it is to be arrested, we must understand the bad choices we have made and discern how the course they set us on can be corrected.

Yet it is not merely America's religious life that is in decline. Most of its other communities are failing as well—families and businesses and neighborhoods and cities and voluntary organizations have all been diminished in recent years. The result is rampant loneliness, a longing for anything that offers some kind of solace, and ultimately a society where the only thing we really share is a desperation for community, and the besetting doubt that we will ever experience those goods.

This book's argument is that these two declines are connected. In part one, we will define the nature and causes of these joint declines, and then draw them together. If we are to reweave the fabric of American common life, we must begin by understanding how it came to be torn in the first place. It is to that task that we now turn.

ONE

THE PASSING OF THE AMERICAN CHURCH

I have this against you, that you have left your first love. Remember therefore from where you have fallen; repent and do the first works, or else I will come to you quickly and remove your lampstand from its place—unless you repent.

REVELATION 2:4-5 (NKJV)

HAVELOCK, THE NEIGHBORHOOD I grew up in and my parents still call home, was historically a working-class railroad town built just northeast of Lincoln, Nebraska, the state capital, in the late nineteenth century. The houses are old and, for the most part, in decent condition even today. Some of the streets are still paved with cobblestones, though the poles and power lines that once lined Touzalin Avenue and powered the trolley have been replaced with narrow islands covered in grass and dotted with modest trees. When I was growing up on Touzalin, I used to tell my parents I'd build a castle on one of those islands, and it would have a walkway—in my mind I pictured a rope bridge—running over Touzalin Avenue, connecting their house to my castle.

There are still neighborhood bars lining Havelock Avenue as well as an old pizza place that has been there since the 1980s and sells the Leaning Tower of Pizza. The pun is a classic Nebraska kind of joke, a wry blend of plainspokenness and dad humor.

It's a surprisingly rough place once you get to know it. A friend who pastors in the neighborhood said to me once that the rest of Lincoln doesn't care about Havelock, and Havelock does not care at all about the rest of Lincoln. Such benign neglect is actually an improvement on the town's historic relationship to its larger neighbor. When the city of Lincoln annexed the old railroad town in the early twentieth century, the enraged citizens stormed the Havelock town hall, seized all the city's records, and had a bonfire on Havelock Avenue. When my parents needed some information about property lines a few years ago before building a privacy fence, they had to pay a surveyor to come out and figure out where exactly the property lines even were. The official records no longer exist.

Havelock may seem like a strange place to start a book about religion, communal life, and alienation in twenty-first-century America. But it's also where I need to begin for the simple reason that Havelock was—and in one sense still is—my home place. I still live within a fifteen-minute drive of the house on Touzalin Avenue, first built in 1910, that my parents have called home since their wedding day in December 1984. Indeed, they got married in their living room. The pictures from the day are still hanging on the walls, fittingly looking down at the room where the wedding happened thirty-five years before.

That home is the first place I learned about community. It is where I took my first steps, said my first words (not until age three, and only after my grandmother called in to the 700 Club to ask Pat Robertson to pray for me), and saw with my own eyes what Christian community was, what it could be, and what it could make. At home I saw a faith that was warm, vibrant, and connected to the stuff of daily life. It was both hopeful and ambitious.

I saw my parents run several ministries out of that house—a Sunday evening boys program, a meal service for families from church, and a youth hockey league. I also saw my mom write an entire kids curriculum from scratch at a computer in my old playroom. In high school I once made a rude remark to my dad about evangelical indifference to the poor. Though he didn't say anything in response to my comment, that December he signed up to ring a bell for the Salvation Army, something he continued to do for over ten years before an injury made it impossible for him to continue. My parents organized a food drive every year for the local homeless shelter, an anomalous act of charity in a church that was otherwise concerned almost entirely with its own life.

The life I knew in Havelock explains in large measure why I am still a Christian. Both in my parents' home and the home of my maternal grandmother, who lived a few blocks away, I found an irresistibly compelling faith. It was devout, joyful, serious, simple, and given to the life of humble, largely invisible service the Scriptures call God's people to.

That hidden fidelity is one picture of Christian faith I have seen.

Here is another, and this is one many of my peers have seen as well, I'm afraid: rampant sexual sin among alleged spiritual leaders, a sneering disdain for fellow believers (to say nothing of non-Christians), and a general lack of concern for the poor and the marginalized, all wrapped up in a shiny outer layer that masks the bones moldering within. I have seen a pastor fired after being caught in an affair, only to have the church turn the pastor's children against their (completely innocent) mother and then arrange for the fired pastor to get a comfortable sales gig that probably paid as much or more than his (not inconsiderable) salary from the church. At the end of it all, they marveled at how "God provided."

I've seen staff members go to prison for sexual misconduct and heard stories of six-figure sums of money "disappearing." Many others have also seen in the church the hypocrisy and pride I came to know so well. Where God calls his people to service, the American church has far too often pursued power. When we ought to have embraced the humble place of penitence, we have instead chased after thrones powered by an inexhaustible confidence in our righteousness. And with each turn of the crank, each step into deeper darkness, many of our leaders have chosen to double down on their vanity rather than face the possibility that they may have sown the wind, that their work may not have been done for God but mostly for themselves. They have become wealthy, powerful, needing nothing—and that is precisely the problem. The simple love of God, the love I saw pictured so vividly in my own home, has often been almost entirely absent from movement evangelicalism.

The disgraced megachurch pastor Mark Driscoll once described his church's growth by saying that there was "a pile of dead bodies behind the Mars Hill bus." As if that wasn't bad enough, he added, "and, by God's grace, it'll be a mountain by the time we're done."[1] Though Mars Hill would close not too many years after Driscoll spoke those awful words, his remarks map quite neatly onto a post-Trumpian evangelicalism that has left behind its first love and instead embraced a gospel of power and wealth. And there is indeed a mountain of bodies in its wake. Many of them are known to me. They're the people I grew up with, people I went to college with, people whose posts I still see pop up occasionally on Facebook.

This book, then, is not simply about the decline of the evangelical church in America, although we must discuss that first. It is about the broader question of how we build flourishing communities shaped by the truths taught in the Christian faith. The goal is not merely to see the faith passed on to our children but also to see others enter the community and similarly be nourished and in time drawn to Christ themselves. And much of that has to do with the question of place, home, and the daily practices that shape *those* places.

Old Testament scholar Walter Brueggemann says that our current crisis is not one of meaninglessness but rootlessness. "There are no meanings apart from roots."[2] As we explore the question of Christian community in a world increasingly set as much against that second word, *community*, as it is the first, *Christian*, we must constantly return to the questions of roots, home, and place, all of which we will explore in more detail later.

Spiritual leaders failed me and many others as well. So did the institutional churches they presided over. But my parents' home never did, and the simple life we had together in Havelock has made all the difference.

THE PASSING OF THE AMERICAN CHURCH

In Scripture we see repeated examples of how God chastens his people after a season of prolonged and unrepentant sin. The Israelites under Moses wandered for forty years in the desert until the generation who rebelled against God at the first attempted entry into Canaan had almost

THE PASSING OF THE AMERICAN CHURCH—15

entirely died off. Later the period of the Judges would be marked by short terms of fidelity followed by far longer times of particularly egregious sin, with each cycle ending with severe judgment passed against Israel. Still later in the Old Testament both the northern and southern kingdoms would be taken into exile as punishment for their idolatry. Time after time, we see this biblical pattern of God's people entering a season of unrepentant sin and being coldly awoken to their state through a particularly severe form of judgment.

There is ample reason to believe that the American church is entering such a season. The shadow of sexual abuse lingers over both the Roman Catholic Church in the United States and the evangelical church. The stories of abuse of minors in Catholic churches has been known for nearly two decades now. That predatory priests and bishops were targeting seminarians as well became more widely known in 2018 as adult victims of predatory clerics came forward across the northeast and in my hometown of Lincoln. Evangelicals are no better on this issue, sadly. Rape victim Jules Woodson came forward and named her attacker, a former youth pastor of hers, Andy Savage. Savage, who had since become a teaching pastor at a prominent megachurch, publicly confessed the sin to his church, while deliberately misrepresenting Woodson's part in it. The church greeted his confession with a standing ovation. The same thing would happen at Willow Creek when Bill Hybels first acknowledged to the congregation the abuse allegations he faced in spring 2018. These failures alone would be sufficient grounds for God to send the American church into exile, and yet they are not our only grievous offenses.

White evangelicals are more likely than any other religious group to support the use of torture.[3] Even after the revelation of President Trump's paid affair with porn star Stormy Daniels, which occurred shortly after the birth of his son Barron, evangelicals continued to support him. Indeed, they were *more* likely to support him in April 2018 than they were in November 2016.[4] One prominent social conservative leader, Tony Perkins of the Family Research Council, even proposed that Trump be given "a mulligan" on the Daniels affair. Needless to say, no prominent evangelical leaders were feeling so forgiving in the 1990s when the occupant of the White House was a Democrat.

On top of the moral hypocrisy, there are other signs of internal rot as well. Public polling on the theological and ethical beliefs of American Catholics is alarming and a testimony to the catechetical failings of the American Roman Catholic Church following the Second Vatican Council. According to the Pew Research Group, a full 89 percent of American Catholics view the use of contraception as being either morally acceptable or not a moral issue despite the clear teachings of the Church on the matter. In fact, American Catholics are more likely than nonreligious Americans to say that using contraceptives is morally acceptable. Similarly, 47 percent of American Catholics say that having an abortion is morally acceptable or not a moral issue.[5] Likewise, a May 2013 Pew study found that 71 percent of American Catholics believe that homosexuality should be morally accepted, another departure from Church teaching. In fact, according to the study, American Catholics are more likely to approve of homosexuality than American mainline Protestants, a famously progressive demographic.[6]

Again, however, the situation among American evangelicals is no better. Consider the famed claim of the mid-2000s that roughly one-third of all Americans were evangelical. That number, along with the Bush presidency, inspired no lack of anxiety among American progressives at the time. But back in 2007 the Barna Group decided to survey those self-described evangelicals to find out what they actually believed theologically.[7] After all, evangelical identity is not merely a matter of self-description. Traditionally it also implies adherence to certain theological ideas. So, do American evangelicals embrace evangelical beliefs?

The answer Barna found is a resounding *no*. The Barna survey found that while 38 percent of Americans identified as evangelical, only 8 percent of Americans affirmed nine key statements, all taken from the National Association of Evangelicals, which Barna used to narrow what was actually meant by the term *evangelical*. Respondents were asked whether they

1. have made a personal commitment to Jesus Christ that is still important in their life today;

2. believe that when they die they will go to heaven because they have confessed their sins and accepted Jesus Christ as Savior;

3. would say their faith is very important in their life;

4. believe they have a personal responsibility to share their religious beliefs with non-Christians;

5. believe that Satan exists;

6. believe salvation is possible only through grace, not works;

7. believe that Jesus lived a sinless life on earth;

8. believe that the Bible is accurate in all it teaches; and

9. would describe God as an all-knowing, all-powerful, perfect deity who created the universe and rules it today.

Here's what that means: In 2007, 82 million Americans said they were evangelical. However, statistically speaking only around 18 million Americans agreed with all nine of those basic theological commitments. That means 64 million self-described American evangelicals rejected at least one of these extremely basic statements about the nature of Christian faith and piety.

To fully capture what that means, we might put it this way: At the same time that George W. Bush was in the White House, that we were talking about a constitutional amendment to ban same-sex marriage, and that progressives were writing panicky books warning about the looming danger of theocracy, we were also overestimating the number of evangelical believers in America by a factor of 4.5. We thought that roughly 38 percent of the nation's population was evangelical. But, theologically speaking, the number was actually more like 8 percent. To be sure, some might argue that one can be culturally evangelical without being theologically evangelical. That said, evangelicalism in particular is at bottom a religious identifier that follows from its affirmation of certain religious doctrines. Cultural evangelicalism is thus not a helpful label.

We looked big and influential on paper. But really we had already been hollowed out by decades of poor catechesis and an alarming tendency to chase worldly fads instead of true Christian discipline. We said, "We are rich; we have prospered, and we need nothing," not realizing that we were wretched, pitiable, poor, blind, and naked (see Revelation 3:17).

HOW HAS THE AMERICAN CHURCH FAILED?

The obvious question to ask is how the American church, which once appeared so strong and robust, could fail so spectacularly. In his book *Bad Religion*, *New York Times* columnist Ross Douthat describes an ascendant American church in the postwar years. This included a vibrant Catholic Church led by figures like Bishop Fulton Sheen, a famous TV evangelist for the Roman Church, and a rising evangelical movement led by the famous traveling preacher Billy Graham. So how did we go from *that* to the current state of the church in what is, historically speaking, a short period of time? How has the American church failed so spectacularly so quickly?

While that may be the question American Christians *want* to ask, it is the wrong question. The American church, Catholic and evangelical alike, has produced politically opportunistic people who are de facto moral relativists and are largely ignorant of the teachings of the faith. Given that, we *could* ask why these movements have failed to produce deeply pious Christians impressed with the image of Christ and given to love of God and neighbor. But it is probably better to ask if these churches were ever designed to produce such a thing in the first place.

In *The Sacrifice of Africa*, the Ugandan Roman Catholic priest and scholar Emmanuel Katongole begins by surveying the state of modern African politics before turning to a familiar trope among many of the continent's observers: why has the political system failed so spectacularly in postcolonial Africa? Katongole's answer to that question is as incisive as it is surprising. "What makes you think it has *failed*?" he asks his readers.

> [Recommendations to improve the existing political systems in Africa] do not pay sufficient attention to the possibility that politics in Africa, and the nation-state in particular, have not been a failure, but have worked very well. Chaos, war, and corruption are not indications of a failed institution; they are ingrained in the very imagination of how nation-state politics works.[8]

In other words, rampant civil war, economic inequality, and failing public institutions may not be proof that politics have failed in sub-Saharan Africa. Rather, they may be proof that the existing political institutions have done what they were designed to do, which is enrich the few and exploit the many. Though the last names of "the few" changed at the end of colonialism, the underlying narrative about politics did not change, and so the results stayed the same. And by the standards of the established political narrative the results were a great success.

Something like this principle holds true for American Christianity as well. The American Catholic Church began to lust after mainstream respectability not long after the end of World War II. Indeed, they rallied to support a candidate for president, John F. Kennedy, who publicly acknowledged that he would not govern according to the teachings of the Church. The speech Kennedy gave in 1960 to Baptist pastors on the separation of church and state aligns well with accepted American beliefs about the separation of church and state, but it is hard to square with the teaching of the Roman Church which has, since the medieval era, held that the pope has authority over both the spiritual realm and the temporal, which includes questions of politics.[9] Yet such was the desire for mainstream acceptability among American Catholics that they found it easier to abandon clear church teaching than to maintain fidelity to the dogma of the Church.

From the 1970s onward, American evangelicalism has been prone to the same errors. At bottom, the recent evangelical movement has been designed to do two things: first, grow churches through innovative worship practices and uncritically adopting the cultural garb of suburban Middle America. Second, to secure political power through an alliance with the Republican Party.[10] These are the programs of the seeker-sensitive movement and the Religious Right, respectively.

Thus the idea that the mass endorsement of President Trump or the ascent of heterodox celebrity pastors whose own moral lives are often disasters would represent *failures* in American evangelicalism is simply disconnected from the reality of the movement.

An old joke can sum up the failure nicely: It's said that Thomas Aquinas was once brought into a great city where he was to meet the pope. He saw huge churches, clerics in ornate garb, and great armies lined up to defend the church's rule. And as he took all this in, the pope looked at him and said, "No more can St. Peter say 'silver and gold have I none,'" referencing the story in Acts 3 where Peter says those words to a lame man begging to be healed. "Indeed," responds Thomas, "but neither can he say, 'rise, take up your bed and walk.'" In the years since World War II the American church has consistently chosen to chase power, prestige, and mainstream status. We have gained all of those things.

The tragedy, of course, is that those are the very things that Jesus warns us about so frequently in the Gospels. A movement designed to obtain power and prestige and status will end up where Jesus predicted it would and where the American church *has* ended up. Modern American Christianity was never intended to produce morally upright people given to sacrificial love of neighbor. If it were intended to do that, we would not continue to restore discredited, unrepentant leaders to roles of authority within the movement.

Consider the aftermath of Tullian Tchvidjian's fall from grace in 2015, after he was caught in an extramarital affair. As the story slowly leaked out it became apparent that the rot ran deep. Tchvidjian had, by then, already been engaged in theological controversy over his views on the law and gospel. Many critics, rightly, called his views "antinomian," which is a Christian heresy that rejects all positive use of the law in the Christian life. Unsurprisingly, moral failure accompanied his aberrant theology. Tchvidjian's wife had actually had an affair before he himself did, and then he had *multiple* affairs. Yet after all of this, the Anglican writer Paul Zahl said of Tchvidjian, "I would go so far as to say that Tullian's personal experience, as bad as you want to make it out, has qualified him (and qualified him brilliantly!) to preach the Gospel."[11]

Tchvidjian, of course, is not the only pastor who has resurfaced after being caught in grave sin. Ted Haggard and the aforementioned Mark Driscoll have followed similar trajectories. Indeed, there is almost a sense in which failures of this sort have become a mark of honor—they prove your authenticity, that you really are human and broken just like the rest of us.

The Catholic Church is, again, no better as the restoration of serial abuser Cardinal Theodore McCarrick under Pope Francis made abundantly clear. The American Catholic Church desired wealth and needed fundraisers to secure that wealth. Both the liberal McCarrick and the conservative Marcial Maciel could use their ability to raise money as a protective armor that allowed them to get away with sexual abuse for decades.

The same lesson applies in politics: American Christians have long adopted the practice of looking the other way when one of their favored political leaders fails. Former governor of South Carolina Mark Sanford took a brief break from politics after the popular Religious Right icon was caught in an extramarital affair. But after only a couple years away, he returned to run for the House of Representatives—and white conservative Christians in South Carolina enthusiastically supported him. Similarly Louisiana politician David Vitter survived scandal after being caught in an extramarital affair. Far from being a surprise, the capitulation to Donald Trump was almost inevitable, particularly when considering the fears that conservative Christians had about the ongoing viability of their dominant institutions.

Far from being evidence of our movement's failure, the current state of American Christianity is proof that our movement has succeeded spectacularly, if by *succeed* we mean "done what it was intended to do."

In the final pages of his great epic *The Lord of the Rings*, J. R. R. Tolkien writes of his heroes, Sam and Frodo, and their desperate quest to reach the cursed Mount Doom to cast the ring of power, a device that held much of the dark lord Sauron's power, into the fires and destroy it. As they came closer to the mountain, their situation grew more desperate. They were wasting away physically, Frodo's spirit was failing, and their quest seemed hopeless. In a key moment, Sam attempts to encourage Frodo by asking him if he remembers the taste of strawberries and cream, the sound of water, the beauties of spring in their far-off home, the Shire. This should be instructive to us. Love of small things, fidelity to small places, these are the things that matter and ultimately enable great deeds of courage.

For Christians, this means an ordinary delight in the created gifts of God should nourish our piety and our daily lives: the look of clouds on a stormy spring day, the delight of a good glass of red wine, the feel of wind blowing against our cheek as we walk in the created world spoken into being by God. It also means delighting in the ordinary means of grace that God offers to us, the preached Word of God, and the blessed sacrament given to us by a generous God who, as Calvin said, accommodates himself to our limitations. A simple life of work and prayer in a particular place among a beloved people is all that God's people need aspire to. And when we aspire to something beyond this hidden fidelity, it doesn't take long for things to go sideways.

Near the end of Wendell Berry's novel *Jayber Crow*, the protagonist, the small-town Kentucky barber the book is named for, asks himself if the many sacrifices he has made and opportunities he has let pass by so that he could live his simple life in a small place were worth it. What did it get him? He answers, "I got to live with love in my heart."

We might say the failure of evangelicalism is that we have forgotten the taste of strawberries and cream, and so have not lived with love in our hearts. And we are now passing into a well-deserved exile.

But even in exile, there is hope.

YEAST WITHOUT STRENGTH

The tragedy of the decline of the American church cannot be limited only to the lives of practicing Christians. The effects reach far beyond that. The Proverbs tell us that when the righteous prosper, the city rejoices. A rising church lifts all boats, you might say.

The martyred El Salvadoran archbishop Oscar Romero understood this well. Citing the parable of the yeast in the dough, Romero said that

> Bakers know how the little bit of yeast that is placed within the dough leavens the entire mass. This is what Christians should be: the smidgens of yeast that go on to transform their families, their neighborhoods, their communities, their towns, the entire country, the world! But now we are yeast without strength, and that is why we have not been able to leaven the mass.[12]

The trouble, of course, is that yeast works quietly and gradually. You must be patient. But American Christians, and evangelicals especially, lack this patience. And it isn't just Christians who suffer as a result. When we turn to the broader question of public life in America, we find that the American republic is faring no better than the American church. Though by some measures the American economy is strong and robust, that strength has primarily benefited a select few. The masses have been left behind. Moreover, there is real reason to worry that the problem may get far worse in the near future as automation threatens what few under-paying jobs still remain for working-class Americans. The largest em-ployer in many states is the trucking industry, and it may prove particu-larly susceptible to automation as self-driving trucks cause truckers to become unemployed and robots and advanced software similarly drive gas station attendants and warehouse workers out of their jobs. That transformation alone could eliminate millions of American jobs.

But the malaise is not purely economic. As noted in the introduction, sociologists have coined a new term, *deaths of despair*, to describe the skyrocketing number of deaths due to suicide, drug overdose, or alco-holism occurring in much of rural America and now beginning to become more common in American cities. Similarly, loneliness is on the rise as three-fourths of Americans report having two or fewer close friends they can share their great joys and anxieties with. Today's American teen is more anxious than ever before. In his inaugural address President Trump spoke of American carnage. There is little reason to think the president understands this carnage in any deep way or that he has a plan to address it. But that it exists is clear to even the most foolish among us, as his address makes plain.

In such a world the Christian church could be a powerful force for good. Liberated Christians, set free to a life of service and sacrifice by the death and resurrection of Christ, could be the glue that holds homes, neighborhoods, and companies together. The great English poet W. H. Auden once said in a letter to a Christian friend that if it were not for "a few like you," he would have been lost to despair. This is the ministry the church could have.

Indeed, one of the tragic ironies of today's evangelicalism particularly is that its theological predecessors, the great Reformers of sixteenth-century Europe, often critiqued the established church precisely because it had become decadent and indifferent to the poor. The Strasbourg Reformer Martin Bucer's first published book was titled *That No One Should Live for Himself but for Others.* Martin Luther raised many similar concerns with the Catholic Church. In his pamphlet "Address to the German Nobility," Luther repeatedly describes how the Roman Catholic Church exploited German peasants to enrich themselves, sending fraudulent preachers like John Tetzel to manipulate the poor into giving money to extravagant church projects. These early evangelicals rightly saw that a Christian faith that wasn't good news for the masses was not good news at all. And they called their followers to reform the Church such that it could, again, proclaim that message so its members would pour themselves out for their neighbors.

The bad news is that for the most part today's American Christians have come to look like the corrupt, self-satisfied, rich Roman Church of the late medieval era. The good news is that even now we can find a few small places where this gospel of self-sacrifice is being embraced and practiced.

In my hometown of Lincoln, the city's largest and most successful homeless shelter is run by a Pentecostal pastor who gave up a lucrative career in the business world to become a minister with the particular goal of loving and helping the poor.

A friend of mine runs a successful architecture firm that employed a number of people prior to the housing collapse in 2008. Even in the midst of that collapse, which saw almost all of the firm's work dry up, my friend paid the salaries of his employees from his personal funds for as long as he could afford to do so. He lost his house in the process, but his employees had a paycheck for far longer than almost anyone else in their field precisely because of the Spirit-empowered generosity of a good Christian man.

One of the best examples of this is the work of John Perkins and the Christian Community Development Association. After being nearly beaten to death by a white policeman during the civil rights movement, Perkins dedicated his life to the work of reconciliation in American cities. The organization he founded, CCDA, has proven instrumental in bringing peace where once there was violence and pain. The organization has grown to nearly ten thousand members and over a thousand partner organizations, most of which work in impoverished urban settings.[13]

Even so, the dominant narrative of our age remains one of decadence, an aimless and meaningless search after wealth and power for no reason save one's own personal peace and affluence, as the evangelist Francis Schaeffer anticipated nearly fifty years ago.[14] The result has been a rending in the fabric of the American republic. In such a time of chaos and mistrust, reconciliation is badly needed. And the church has, Scripture tells us, been given precisely such a ministry.

But the story of reconciliation runs counter to not only the story currently ascendant in America but the story that has for too long been dominant in the American church. Because we have mostly forgotten that in God's economy the way up is the way down, we have been too eager to measure ourselves by worldly standards of success and therefore have forgotten the story told in Scripture of God's people. In that story we are told that God's people are brought to life by God and called to a certain sort of life in his world. In their book *Reconciling All Things*, Emmanuel Katongole and Chris Rice tell this alternative story well:

> There are two movements in [the Christian] story and the order is important. The first movement is about God and what God has done in Christ. The second is about the transformation this first movement has enacted in the world and in the lives of people.
>
> Already we see that one way of misreading this story about reconciliation is to immediately bring ourselves into the picture. In our action-infected world, we are tempted to first ask what we must do, jumping into action without dwelling on the gift God gives. But the story of 2 Corinthians 5 reminds us that before reconciliation is about us, it is about God. It is God's mission in the world.[15]

They continue later,

> We begin by attending to the story of God. We remember it in worship.
> We tell it to our children. We memorize its most poignant phrases and ask
> where God wants to speak them again through us. . . . Because a Christian
> vision of reconciliation is rooted in the story of God's people, we can grasp
> the vision only as we learn to inhabit the story. The story shapes us in the
> habits of God's peculiar people; the more we get it down inside us, the
> easier it is to resist the temptations of this world's prevailing visions.[16]

And this brings me back to Havelock. The gift I received there was a
picture that told me in no uncertain terms that nothing was more important than loving Jesus. And loving Jesus did not mean a life of comfort
and wealth; it meant a life of sacrifice and difficulty, but also of beauty
and joy. I grew up on stories of beloved family members who exemplified
the quiet virtues of Christian love.

My grandfather Bert worked a blue-collar railroad job for thirty-five
years to support a sick wife and his three kids. On one occasion, he was
caught between two boxcars and broke several ribs. But he didn't have
any saved time off and so the next day he was back on the job. His family
needed him. Mom tells me she never once heard him complain. This is
a picture of Christian sacrifice, of the quiet fidelity of an ordinary man
who blessed his family and his neighborhood with his constancy.

My great-grandmother Elise, who we met in the introduction, was an
immigrant farmwife living on rented land in the early twentieth century,
married to an admirable Swedish man who worked hard but was prone
to bouts of depression. You already heard about his first suicide attempt
the night before their wedding. It was not his last. In the mid-1920s he
went out on a stormy night and used a ladder to climb up a power plant
near Oakland. From the ladder he grabbed an exposed wire. The shock
nearly killed him, and it caused all the power in the town to go out. In
the aftermath of that attempt on his life, Grandma Elise cared for the
entire family and the farm, making sure that the boys (including a young
grandpa Bert) did the farm work that their father was not able to do
while he was recovering. And through it all she maintained a rich devotional life. Bert could recall till the day he died the sight of his mother

sitting quietly in a rocking chair as he came downstairs at sunrise to begin chores. She was reading her Bible and singing beloved hymns in her native Swedish. Elise held a family together through her simple faith in God. And her descendants are still feeling the impact of that nearly one hundred years later.

My mother has taken care of my dad, who suffered a traumatic brain injury in December 2015, round the clock ever since that awful day. Dad spent two weeks in a coma in the ICU after a drug complication caused a massive bleed on his brain, which caused his brain to actually shift eight centimeters inside his skull. Doctors told us he may not make it, and not long before he miraculously woke up one doctor suggested that we begin planning a funeral.

But Dad woke up.

For me and everyone who knows my parents, the past several years have been an extended object lesson in the patient endurance of the Christian, the call to a life of sacrifice for the good of the beloved, and the steady hope in a future resurrection. About a year after his injury, my parents were talking and realized that they had both come to a similar conclusion about Dad's injury: through their suffering they had gained more than they had lost. Dad had mostly lost the use of his left hand, lost virtually all of his independence, and lost the ability to hunt and to work around the house. Mom lost much of her independence as well. And they both lost a good bit of money as their sole source of income became the combined benefits of an employer provided long-term disability plan and state-provided Social Security payments. And yet for all that, they both saw that the things they gained through that difficulty, most notably a greater dependence on God and a deeper patience and love for God's people, somehow exceeded what they had lost.

This call to hidden fidelity does not mean there are no broader ramifications of the Christian faith. I have already said that there are. But it means a church that loses hidden faith will not be able to sustain public faith. It will, rather, become what the Pharisees were in Jesus' own day— whitewashed tombs, cups scrubbed clean on the outside but filthy on the inside. Scripture teaches us plainly that "man looks on the outward appearance, but God looks on the heart" (1 Samuel 16:7 NKJV) The failure of the American church is that we have become indifferent to the heart. This is because fidelity of the heart will compel us toward an external fidelity that is frequently uncomfortable, demanding, and dangerous.

At a funeral Mass for a friend of Archbishop Romero who was murdered by the government because of her faith in Christ, Romero invited those present to follow this Lord who died, this God who sacrificed himself for others, this obscure Israelite teacher who, we confess, is the hope of the world. Holding the host aloft, he said, "May this body that was immolated and this flesh that was sacrificed for humankind also nourish us so that we can give our bodies and our blood to suffering and pain, as Christ did, not for our own sake but to bring justice and peace to our people."[17]

Moments later a shot echoed through the chapel.

Romero fell to the ground. He was dead within minutes.

But the gospel tells us that a life sacrificed for others yields a crop. "He who loves his life will lose it, and he who hates his life in this world will keep it for eternal life" (John 12:25 NKJV).

TWO

THE UNWINDING
OF COMMON LIFE
IN AMERICA

IN THE FILM *OF GODS AND MEN*, director Xavier Beauvois tells the story of a small group of mostly French monks living in Algeria during a time of civil unrest. These monks live a life of quiet fidelity dedicated to prayer and work in the rural part of the country near a small village. As part of their work, the monks run a small health clinic and also provide necessary physical supplies like clothing and shoes to the people in the village. Early in the film, word reaches the monks that a group of Muslim radicals is on the move and will soon be in the town adjacent to the monastery. The monks will be in danger as soon as the radicals take the town. However, they are given a choice. Because the radicals have not yet arrived, there is time for the monks to leave the monastery and move to a more secure place. In a pivotal scene, the monks speak with members of the village, most of whom are Muslim, about the decision. One monk says that they are all like birds on the branch of a tree, uncertain as to whether or not they will fly away or stay. A woman from the village corrects him. "You are the tree. We are the birds. If you leave, we will lose our footing." I am reminded of the words of Psalm 1, which liken the righteous to a tree with deep roots. The life of the Christian community and the life of the *commonwealth*, a word traditionally favored by Christians to describe the sum total of communal life in a given place, are knitted together. And so the monks make the brave choice to stay. They cannot turn their backs on the people they have been called to.

In chapter one, drawing on the work of Emmanuel Katongole, we saw that communities form around stories and understand themselves through those stories. This was true for these monks: their small community of celibate men was shaped by the Christian story. They knew they were called to a life of prayer, to love of neighbor, to humility. They knew this was the good life and the life God had called them to. Certainly, this was a brave life. But, given the story they believed about the world, it was also an entirely reasonable action. Because of the way God made the world and because of what God had done for them, it followed that they would stay, that they would serve the village, and so on.

That, in short, is a Christian story about community. It tells us that people are naturally gregarious, even naturally political, and so the friendships and institutions and societies we form with one another are both natural and good. Indeed, these stories are themselves a further enacting of the story of God's love for the world, which is the foundation of the Christian faith. God loved us, and so we now love one another, even to the point of sacrificing our own needs for the good of the other. And when we do this, we discover that, as Christ said, "those who lose their lives will find them."

This can all seem banal and simple, of course. Much of the monks' work was gardening, cleaning, and the like. Their pleasures seem similarly small—listening to a symphony while enjoying a simple meal, laughing with friends about old stories, watching kids from the village playing soccer. Much of our work and our delight will probably be similar—preparing a meal for our family, tutoring at-risk youth through an after-school program, enjoying a potluck dinner with friends from church. It all seems small. But if we spend time thinking about it, we'll realize it most certainly isn't.

The delight we experience over the course of ordinary life together is connected to the Christian story. Once we *assume* that we naturally belong to one another, naturally form communities, and therefore must naturally set aside our own personal ambitions for the life of the group, then we create the space in which rich friendship can grow and thrive.

To put it another way, the sites of our life together, whether it is a home, neighborhood, or park, may not appear to be explicitly Christian themselves, but they are nonetheless the product of a basic Christian sensibility about the world. Because it is not good for me to be alone, I will work with my neighbors to create a place where I and others can be together and enjoy one another.

Viewed this way, Christianity is not, as is often thought, some set of individual principles a person can try out if they want to find a greater sense of meaning and purpose in their life. It's actually a true account of the basic nature of reality. It tells us how the world works and how we work and why. It tells us why we long for friendship and how friendship can be sustained. It tells us why we can almost hear the laughter of God himself in the laughter of beloved friends gathered together for a long-anticipated reunion. This is what we humans are made to do; this is the way the world *works*.

From this point follows another. The moral precepts that follow from these specific claims made by Christianity are not optional practices meant to help enrich an individual Christian's personal experience. They are, rather, moral norms that follow from claims about the basic nature of reality. Paul himself is quite clear on this. Everything we can say about Christianity is only valid if Christ did indeed rise from the dead. If he did not, Christians are wasting their time. "We are of all people most to be pitied," is how Paul puts it (1 Corinthians 15:19). But if he *did* rise, then that simple, revolutionary fact changes everything not only for individuals but also for neighborhoods, businesses, cities, nations, and even creation itself.

Christian morality, then, is simply *human* morality. If it isn't, then it's not just the moral claims of Christianity we should dispense with but the other historical and theological claims as well. Christianity's moral norms are based on the idea that there is a way people are meant to function in the world. There is a way of living that goes with the grain of creation, we might say, just as there is a way of cutting a piece of wood that goes with the grain and a way that runs against it (and ruins the saw in the process). To be sure, you don't need to actually understand all of this, let alone mentally assent to all aspects of Christianity, in order to experience this joy any more than you need to understand how electricity works to benefit from electric light and air conditioning. Much of the benefit we experience is so folded into reality that we do not even notice it—until it is gone.

In chapter one we saw that we live in a time of widespread infidelity in the American church. We saw that the church has an idolatrous relationship to political power and a lack of faith in God to work using the ordinary means he has always used throughout church history. We have taken matters into our own hands, "walked by the light of our own sparks," to use a phrase Edith Schaeffer liked. And, as predicted by the verse Schaeffer was alluding to, it has led to us collapsing, lying down in misery beneath the judgment of God.

The tragedy is that when the church fails to preach the gospel faithfully and submit its life to the lordship of Christ, the effects are not limited to the church. Religious life and common life decline together. Pope John Paul II put the problem well when he said, "When the sense of God is lost, the sense of man is also threatened and poisoned."[1]

Christ said we are salt—a preservative that also enhances flavor. But, Jesus asked, "What happens when the salt loses its saltiness?"

We're finding out.

THE MEMORY OF COMMUNITY

There is a scene in the film version of *Harry Potter and the Prisoner of Azkaban* that many of us can relate to. In it, Harry is looking at an old photo of his parents with his godfather, Sirius Black. Sirius runs his finger along the surface of the photo, pointing to the various people in it and explaining their relationship to Harry. But because of the wizarding wars, many of the people in that photo are now dead. They were once important people in the life of Harry's family, and now they are gone. Most of us do not have stories quite this dramatic, of course, but the experience of looking at old photos and seeing friends you haven't spoken to in years is a familiar one for many Americans. It's not that we've always been lonely but we could not *maintain* our communities due to a variety of different challenges set before us.

It is common to hear people lament the absence of stable community and the many attendant social ills that coincide with such an absence. But the problem for most of us is *not* an absolute absence of community, as if we have never known close friends, never been cared for freely by someone we are bound to by affection rather than a contract. We *have* experienced those things, or many of us have at least. Rather, the problem is that such relationships are hard to sustain. We remember a bygone past, our childhood or perhaps high school or college, when we *did* have close friends that we saw regularly and shared life with.

We just don't see much of them anymore.

A NATION OF STRANGERS

Theoretically, the simplest form of community we have would come from the people who live closest to us. They are the people we see every day without needing to make plans to do so. They are the easiest people to ask for help when we need it. They're the people we go to when we need to borrow some sugar for a baking project or are headed out of town and need someone to get our mail and water our plants.

In modern America, we barely know them.

This problem in particular is well-documented, dating all the way back to the late 1990s when sociologist Robert Putnam published a paper on membership in various local communities, which would turn into his now famous book *Bowling Alone*, published in 2000. In the book Putnam examined the decline of various American institutions that helped knit communities together and provided people with stability, purpose, meaning, and direction. Putnam coined a term to describe the value these communities create: *social capital*.[2]

Social capital refers to the accumulated benefits that come from neighbors knowing one another, caring for one another, and having a variety of opportunities to be neighborly toward each other. To make it more concrete, it's referring to the relational benefits that come from neighbors knowing each other well enough to pop over to say hello without any other reason to explain their visit. These things are seemingly small and trivial, but their absence has a significant effect on our quality of life.

Documenting everything from church attendance to neighborhood stability to membership in bowling leagues, where the book drew its title from, Putnam arrived at a single alarming conclusion: America's social capital was being rapidly depleted. The term *capital* is telling—in this understanding, communal life is a bit like a bank account. When we participate in public life, when we serve our neighbors, involve ourselves in voluntary organizations, attend church, and so on, we are adding funds to the account. When we need assistance or draw on the resources of those organizations, we are making withdrawals from the account. In a healthy society, most people have accounts that are in the black, as it were, meaning that they are putting more into their local community through acts of service and simply being available to others than they are taking out. And if our account is in the black, that means that when a real crisis hits, we're able to draw on that capital to help us through it.

My own family has experienced the benefits of social capital. After my dad suffered a traumatic brain injury in winter 2015, friends from their old church they had known and loved for over thirty years banded together to build a wheelchair ramp for their front porch and to make their downstairs bathroom handicap accessible. They put in dozens, perhaps hundreds, of hours of labor, and they did it all for practically nothing— "we accept payment in cookies and Mountain Dew," is what one of the men told my mom. The kindness of those friends saved my parents tens of thousands of dollars and may well be the main reason they were able to stay in their home after dad's injury. *That* is social capital. You spend years upon years knowing other people, and the result is that when one member of the group is in trouble, you all know each other so well and are so close that it is as if the one person's pain is actually distributed across the group.

Putnam's book, written way back during the Clinton administration, raised the concern that more and more Americans had social capital accounts in the red, and as that became more normal the intensity of the problem would grow as there were fewer people with large surpluses to compensate for those carrying large debts. In other words, we would become a nation of people who occasionally have great social needs but no relationships, no friendships, no stable local communal institutions to help meet those needs. We would, instead, become a nation of strangers.

In the twenty years since the book's release, the problems have become more pronounced, just as Putnam feared they would. In 2006, sociologists from Duke and Arizona released a study on loneliness in America. They found that around half of all Americans have two or fewer confidantes they can talk with about their deepest desires or greatest fears. In fact, a quarter of Americans said they did not have a single person they could have such conversations with.[3] That was 2006. In the thirteen years since then, the problem has gotten worse. A 2018 Cigna study found that nearly half of Americans report "sometimes or always feeling alone." Forty-seven percent of Americans also say they do not have meaningful in-person social interactions, such as an extended conversation with a friend or quality time with family, on a daily basis. The scary thing is that the emerging generation, Generation Z, is the loneliest generation of them all.[4]

The health effects of loneliness deserve special mention here. One study found that loneliness affects both physical and mental health in ways comparable to the damage done by smoking fifteen cigarettes per day.[5] Other studies have found links between loneliness and diabetes, heart disease, and depression, and have said that loneliness may also be linked to substance abuse and can in some cases even lead to an early death.[6]

TECHNOLOGY AND COMMUNITY

One strategy that many have proposed for dealing with loneliness and isolation is to use various techniques for helping people to be more available to each other. The assumption is that our problem is ultimately mechanistic in nature—fixing it simply requires finding the right tool or right part required to fix the machine. Thus we are lonely simply because the world has changed and the tools that used to help us feel connected, a neighborhood or a church perhaps, no longer do. But if we can find the right tools to do that same task for our day, then we will be fine. One of the largest businesses in America—Facebook—is theoretically designed to fight against this problem. CEO Mark Zuckerberg said in January 2018, "We built Facebook to help people stay connected and bring us closer together with the people that matter to us."[7]

But Facebook is not the only company that promises to do that. Other social networks, like Twitter and Instagram, are also designed with similar objectives. It's not hard to understand why many think these networks might be the remedy to our loneliness or at least part of the remedy. Thanks to social media networks, I can have instant access to my friends anytime I want via the small device in my pocket. What could be better for helping me to connect with friends and other loved ones? But is that how it works in practice?

According to a story in NPR, the answer is, "not really." Here is the key paragraph:

> It turns out that the people who reported spending the most time on social media—more than two hours a day—had twice the odds of perceived social isolation than those who said they spent a half hour per day or less on those sites. And people who visited social media platforms most frequently, 58 visits per week or more, had more than three times the odds of perceived social isolation than those who visited fewer than nine times per week.[8]

In a piece for *The Atlantic*, social scientist Jean Twenge looked at how various activities, some screen-based and some nonscreen-based, affected happiness among American teens. "There's not a single exception. All screen activities are linked to less happiness, and all nonscreen activities are linked to more happiness."[9] Later in the same essay, Twenge calls today's teens "a lonely, dislocated generation." Twenge is not the only one to say so. In a feature for the *New York Times*, Benoit Denizet-Lewis reported on the growing issues with anxiety afflicting American young people. According to Denizet-Lewis, the number of hospital admissions for suicidal teens doubled between 2007 and 2017. Denizet-Lewis also considered the role of social media and tech in contributing to American struggles with loneliness and anxiety. His own findings agreed with those of Twenge and others.

> Anxious kids certainly existed before Instagram, but many of the parents I spoke to worried that their kids' digital habits—round-the-clock responding to texts, posting to social media, obsessively following the filtered exploits of peers—were partly to blame for their children's struggles. To my surprise, anxious teenagers tended to agree.[10]

The problem with the view that loneliness can be cured through technology is simple: it is based on ideas about human beings that are manifestly untrue. The right tool or part solves a problem when you're dealing with a machine. If I have a program on my computer that isn't doing what I want it to do, I can use some kind of tool to make it do what I want.

But that isn't actually how human beings work. We are creatures, not machines. So assuming that our loneliness is essentially a mechanical bug that can be fixed via a new means of communicating with friends from a distance, as if the chief problem of loneliness is a lack of disembodied communication with other humans, is simply to misunderstand the problem. As human creatures, we want to share our lives with other people. We want our lives to have witnesses. And witnessing another person's life requires more than simply sending them strings of letters via an electronic device. It requires time. It requires physical presence. It requires affection.

Indeed, the sad irony of the technical answer to the problem of loneliness is that in many cases it actually makes the problem worse. The technique we have invented for fixing the problem—social networking via smartphones—ends up having the effect of pulling us even more out of our physical spaces than we already are.

Consider the familiar scene of a family at dinner with each member only half paying attention to one another as they constantly glance down to check their phones. Social media and smartphones make it easier for us to ignore our actual neighbors even as we theoretically use them to combat loneliness.

After all, we don't notice the person sitting across from us on the bus if our head is buried in our phone. We don't see our children playing at the park if we're swiping through our Facebook feed. We don't notice the attempts at conversation over dinner if we are too busy Instagramming our meal for our followers. These technologically mediated encounters with other human beings do not have the immanence and immediacy of face-to-face conversation, but they also do not have the awkwardness that sometimes comes with such conversation and is a necessary part of getting to know another person. MIT scholar Sherry Turkle has written extensively about this problem in her books *Alone Together* and *Reclaiming the Lost Art of Conversation*. Megan Garber makes the distinction between social media conversation and face-to-face conversation helpfully in an *Atlantic* feature on Turkle's work.

> Conversations, as they tend to play out in person, are messy—full of pauses and interruptions and topic changes and assorted awkwardness. But the messiness is what allows for true exchange. It gives participants the time—and, just as important, the permission—to think and react and glean insights. "You can't always tell, in a conversation, when the interesting bit is going to come," Turkle says. "It's like dancing: slow, slow, quick-quick, slow. You know? It seems boring, but all of a sudden there's something, and whoa."
>
> Occasional dullness, in other words, is to be not only expected, but celebrated. Some of the best parts of conversation are, as Turkle puts it, "the boring bits." In software terms, they're features rather than bugs.
>
> The logic of conversation as it plays out across the Internet, however—the into-the-ether observations and the never-ending feeds and the many, many selfies—is fundamentally different, favoring showmanship over exchange, flows over ebbs. The Internet is always on. And it's always judging you, watching you, goading you. "That's not conversation," Turkle says.[11]

What we are longing for today is the experience of being in the presence of another person and feeling known and accepted. But that feeling is not something that can be mediated via pixels on a screen. It must be conveyed through the many other forms of communication that influence conversation—body language, tone, facial expressions—these are the things that make human conversation *human*. They are the things that help to assure us we are seen. You cannot simply remove these factors from human relationships and retain normal, healthy human friendships.

Far from being the answer to our struggle to love and be loved, the ascent of social media and ubiquitous smartphones seem to have made the problems that already existed even more pronounced and challenging.

THE SPLINTERING OF THE FAMILY

Our loneliness has other effects as well. Consider one of the chief weapons in the battle against loneliness: family. Because we have become so isolated from one another, it is now much harder to form families. Household formation is both delayed and in plain decline among younger Americans. After all, how can we meet people and form households if we are all mostly lonely and alienated from one another? Online dating can fill in some of the gap created by the erosion of smaller communities, but it is likely not coincidental that the most successful online dating apps seem set up to encourage one-night hookups rather than long-term relationships. Apps like Tinder are set up to treat potential partners in the same way products are treated on a popular e-commerce site like Amazon. Here is a picture. Do you want to consume this person? By both emphasizing the abundance of potential partners and reducing those partners to a limited set of qualities, many (though not all) dating apps encourage a consumer mindset in relationships that will inevitably privilege hookups and sideline long-term fidelity. The result of this breakdown is that one of the relationships that could most help us fight against the damages done by loneliness is, at best, delayed to much later in life and in more tragic cases becomes inaccessible to many. A 2014 *Rolling Stone* story provides a harrowing account of romantic relationships among younger Americans that demonstrates how this consumptive mentality manifests itself in a variety of ways.[12]

The typical American male now marries for the first time at age twenty-nine, and women marry for the first time at age twenty-seven.[13] Delayed marriage typically also means the couple has fewer children simply due to a lack of time to have them combined with the fact that both members are typically further into their careers and stepping away from work in order to have a family, as many women in particular will have to do, is difficult. Additionally, unfriendly workplaces and paid leave policies in American businesses are further disincentives to having children. The result is that the American birthrate has dropped dramatically, falling to 1.76 births per woman on average and an overall number of 60.2 births per 1,000 woman—a 50 percent drop from what it was in 1970.[14]

Both Putnam and Charles Murray have painted a frightening picture of what this breakdown will mean for our nation's children and for our common life more generally. After charting the decline of children living in a home with both biological parents, Murray writes,

> No matter what the outcome being examined—the quality of the mother-infant relationship, externalizing behavior in childhood (aggression, delinquency, and hyperactivity), delinquency in adolescence, criminality as adults, illness and injury in childhood, early mortality, sexual decision making in adolescence, school problems and dropping out, emotional health, or any other measure of how well or poorly children do in life—the family structure that produces the best outcomes for children, on average, are two biological parents who remain married.[15]

Putnam in particular worries that a large gap has opened up between rich American children and American children from working-class backgrounds. In the latter case, the combination of instability and lack of opportunity has created a stagnation among America's poor that can quickly lead to despair. Indeed, the subtitle of Putnam's most recent book, *Our Kids*, is significant: *The American Dream in Crisis*. For both Putnam and Murray, this crisis facing our nation's children is not simply a problem that will be with us today, it is a problem that will continue to affect our country long into the future.

Meanwhile, journalist Jonathan Last has noted that our falling fertility numbers will create other problems in the coming decades. The most significant problem that comes with an aging population is that just as the cost of care for the elderly is beginning to skyrocket due to an aging population, the working tax base, which pays payroll taxes to help fund those services, is shrinking. So demand for elder care grows at the same time that the pot of money to fund that care shrinks.[16]

There is also a spiritual cost to having fewer children in a society. The innocence and simple delight with which healthy children engage the world has a beneficial effect on all of us. A video from a UK-based group called the Campaign to End Loneliness made the point well. The video producers took young children into coffee shops in the United Kingdom and simply asked them to go around and talk to people. Some of the results are both endearing and heartbreaking. In one exchange, a young girl sits down with an aging man and begins by asking him why he has white hair. Eventually the talk turns more serious: she asks him if he has friends. "Well, I've had hundreds and thousands of friends. At the moment I have a lot of Facebook friends," he says. The girl then, in a moment of innocence that we encounter only in children responds, "I think everybody should talk to everybody." At the end of the video, another girl says, "Making friends is easier than eating chocolate."[17] The innocence these children bring, the simple joy in the givenness of what has been set before them, is often lacking when we do not have as many children around.

Lutheran pastor Hans Fiene made a similar point in a brief note published online in 2018. Writing to parents who are worried about having children in church because of the sounds they make, Fiene said,

> For many years, there were no little children at River of Life Lutheran Church (LCMS). And throughout all those years, the saints of River of Life prayed that God would bless us to see families with little ones walk in our doors. So when we hear little ones squawking and fussing and crying on Sunday mornings, we're not irritated or frustrated. We're overjoyed. Because that's the sound of our prayers being answered. And I know my congregation is not alone in thinking this way.[18]

In this sense, the dystopian novel for our day might not be the oft-cited *1984* or *Brave New World* or even Margaret Atwood's *Handmaid's Tale*. It may well be P. D. James's early 1990s novel *The Children of Men*, which was adapted to the big screen in a film directed by Alfonso Cuarón and starring Clive Owen in 2006. *The Children of Men* is set in a world in which people have stopped having babies entirely. No one knows why. No experiments to find a cure have succeeded. For eighteen years, there have been no new babies. The results are social breakdown as human beings fail to see the point in building things if nothing can be passed on. Charlie Clark summarized the problem in a review of James's novel:

> The *Children of Men* proposes that in the absence of any legacy, many of the ordinary and healthy patterns of human life lose their meaning and appeal. Succeeding generations, whether direct descendants or not, are essential to a meaningful legacy. Consider how many elders have no substantial inheritance to pass on to the next generation, whether because proletarianization has left them without property or because technological disruption has rendered old knowledge apparently worthless.[19]

None of this should surprise us, of course. The Scriptures frequently speak of children as a blessing. They are in themselves a sort of incarnation of human love, an enactment of love walking about in the world. And we should not be surprised that a society with fewer of them is a less healthy society.

THE PROFESSIONALIZATION OF DAILY CARE

One consequence of this creeping loneliness and our inability to solve it is that many of us instinctively feel the need to turn to other people for help. And yet because we have become so isolated, we do not have friends or family to call on. Instead, we must turn to various professionals who can now be counted on to fill the roles once held by the organic communities we were born into. A 2010 paper for the Hoover Institution, published by Ronald Dworkin, highlights how rapid and extreme the transformation has been.[20]

In the 1940s, there were 2,500 clinical psychologists, 30,000 social workers, and fewer than 500 marriage and family therapists working in the United States. By 2010, only seventy years later—roughly one human lifetime—those numbers had skyrocketed. We now had 77,000 clinical psychologists, 192,000 clinical social workers, 400,000 nonclinical social workers, 50,000 marriage and family therapists, 105,000 mental health counselors, 220,000 substance-abuse counselors, 17,000 nurse psychotherapists, and 30,000 life coaches.

Put another way, though the US population grew by 134 percent between 1940 and 2010, the number of service and therapeutic professionals fulfilling basic life needs rose by 3,206 percent. To be sure, some of that growth is explained by greater awareness of particular life situations and mental illnesses that make psychological care necessary. We have shifted, mostly for the better, in how we understand mental health and now offer better care to those afflicted by mental illness. Moreover, we also have a more robust safety net to protect vulnerable populations. To whatever extent the increase is explainable by those things, it is a welcome development. Even so, a 3,000-plus percent spike is remarkable and suggestive of both deeper social issues and the absence of other providers of routine daily care.

Writing of this problem in the *Atlantic*, Stephen Marche observed, "This raft of psychic servants is helping us through what used to be called regular problems. We have outsourced the work of everyday caring."[21] After all, if you live close to your parents, have several trusted friends, and are also involved in a local church and are known to members and to the pastor, much of the help provided by therapists and life coaches may simply be addressed in the course of day-to-day life over conversation with those people. Because we do not have *those* people, we now avail ourselves more frequently of life coaches and therapists.

THE DESPAIR OF MODERN AMERICA

Given this crippling loneliness that besets our nation, the following statistics are tragically predictable. Since 1990 the number of drug overdose deaths in the United States has increased 500 percent.[22] Additionally, the suicide rate went up 21 percent from 2006, when it was 10.97/100,000 people, to 2015, when it had jumped to 13.26/100,000 people.[23]

The dangers of this drug epidemic may become only more acute in the years to come. As explained in books such as J. D. Vance's *Hillbilly Elegy*, drug addiction often coincides with the hollowing out of rural communities. Indeed, the communities hardest hit by the drug epidemic are mostly in rural areas, although there is reason to think the opioid crisis is beginning to come to cities as well.

According to a report in the *Charleston Gazette Mail*, drug companies sold 780 million painkiller pills in West Virginia in only six years.[24] There are only two million people in West Virginia—that's 390 pills per person. It's not just the Rust Belt and old mining country being rocked by this epidemic though. Rather, we can generally correlate drug addiction rates with regional poverty rates. Drug addiction is a devastating scourge in the aforementioned regions, but it has also hit other impoverished parts of America quite hard. In Manatee County, Florida, 41 percent of deaths in the 15 to 44 age range are drug related. In Grant County, New Mexico, that number is 47 percent. In Dickinson County, Michigan, it is 34 percent.[25]

This is the America we live in today. Thus, it is not simply Christian community that is in danger but the very notion of community. The crisis is not one of an ascendant secularism prepared to batter Christianity into oblivion. It is rather one of a comprehensive social breakdown that leaves no corner of life untouched, no person immune to its effects. What we are seeing is a comprehensive crisis of public life. It isn't just the church that is under threat. Havelock, Nebraska, is too. The church has forgotten its calling. The tree is dying. And society, like the bird in *Of Gods and Men*, is losing its footing.

PART TWO

THE

PROBLEMS

FOR

COMMUNITY

IN THE FIRST TWO CHAPTERS we focused on two basic points: First, religious life is in decline in America and the American church has proven largely incapable of responding to this decline effectively. Too often the church has chosen short-term strategies that protect the status quo for a short while longer rather than soberly assessing the problem and making the potentially radical changes necessary to address it. Second, the common life of the United States—families, neighborhoods, small businesses, voluntary organizations, and so on—are failing. We do not know our neighbors and are desperately lonely. We are anxious. We are economically insecure. We delay family formation, if we ever get around to it at all. The result: we are beset by despair. These two declines exist together. Religious life and common life cannot be understood apart from one another.

In this section, we'll move from the more theoretical analysis of the opening chapters to develop a concrete picture of what our life together looks like today in the United States. Specifically, we will consider the dominant social story that is told in contemporary America and see how the contours of that story promise something they are unable to deliver, leaving those who listen to the story worse off in the end.

Every social narrative that a culture or people embraces is trying to do a relatively basic thing: tell them how they can have meaningful work to do with people they care about. Three questions are inherent in that task: How do we live meaningful lives? How do we form communities? What work do we attempt together in those communities?

In this section, I will outline how the modernist story, which is the dominant narrative in the United States today, answers those questions. I will define what the modernist story is, how it tells us to find meaning in life, how it tells us to build communities, and how it structures the work that we do.

THREE

THE LOSS OF MEANING

IN PIXAR'S 2008 FILM *WALL-E* WE MEET a small robot whose only job is to clean up trash. The robot, Wall-E, spends his days rolling around on an entirely abandoned planet earth, slowly cleaning up mounds and mounds of garbage. Why is the earth empty? Due to the amount of energy humanity used and the trash it created, they essentially destroyed organic life on the planet. To save humanity, the world's largest corporation, a grocer and retailer called Buy-N-Large (BNL), created spaceships where the small number of fortunate people who escaped the planet now live. What are those survivors doing? They mostly sit in self-piloting hover chairs that move them from amusement to amusement on the BNL spaceships. The chairs come outfitted with a device that projects a small screen, which provides all the same services as a smartphone, in front of the chair's user. If a person wants food or a drink, they simply speak and a small robot brings it to them.

The result of this lifestyle, of course, is not only that people have grown obese, but also that there are hundreds of people floating alongside each other but never actually even noticing the other, let alone speaking with each other face-to-face. When Wall-E inadvertently disrupts this routine and speaks to them, the response is a kind of pleasant confusion—people slowly respond by introducing themselves before looking around the room and noticing, as if for the first time, the place they are in.

The theme at the heart of the movie is that the love between two robots, Wall-E and EVE (note the not-particularly-subtle name), reminds the people aboard the ship of who they are and what the good life actually is. They had grown distant from one another. The robots, on the other hand, are actually much more human than the people. What makes them more human is their concern for serving one another, for giving up their own comfort for the sake of the beloved. In a world where the whole point of one's existence is *to be comfortable*, the testimony of their actions is jarring to their observers.

The dominant story these unfortunate people had lived with, mediated to them by Buy-N-Large and its army of robots and shelves upon shelves of cheap goods, had caused them to forget. They were free to consume, free to go where they pleased (they even had technology to help them get there more easily), and free to explore the galaxy. Every obstacle to comfort had been removed. And yet, somehow, this freedom didn't look all that free. The story BNL told them was one of freedom and autonomy. The lived reality of that story was quite another.

SOCIETIES AND CULTURES ARE PRODUCTS OF STORIES

Communities are products of stories. Stories help us identify heroes and villains, to attach a sense of greater meaning to the banal events of daily life. They give us the conviction that we are in some sense on an adventure right now, working toward the realization of some long-hoped-for dream. Duke theologian Stanley Hauerwas explains it well in his essay about the novel *Watership Down*, arguing that, "The essential tie between politics and adventure not only requires recognition of the narrative nature of politics, but it also reminds us that good politics requires the development of courage and hope as central virtues for its citizens."[1]

If we want to understand the breakdown and isolation described in chapter two, we need to understand the story our society has told itself for many decades now and how that story of emancipation has actually produced alienation.

Though many people have made an attempt at defining what our story is and what its core beliefs are, no one has summarized it more accurately or concisely than former Supreme Court Associate Justice Anthony Kennedy in his ruling in the justly infamous Supreme Court case of *Planned Parenthood v. Casey*.

The case could have overturned *Roe v. Wade*, the Supreme Court case that made abortion legal nationwide, but in a surprise decision the Republican appointee Kennedy sided with the court's liberal justices, writing a decision that gave the legal victory to Planned Parenthood. The way Kennedy argues is striking. In the decision, he argued that, "At the heart of liberty is the right to define one's own concept of existence, of meaning, of the universe, and of the mystery of human life."[2] According to Kennedy, one is not free if one is not able to privately choose "one's own concept of existence, of meaning." Kennedy's idea has older precursors, of course.

French philosopher Jean-Jacques Rousseau, for example, argued that society was inherently alienating and repressive because it forced us to assume roles for ourselves that we would not otherwise have chosen— thus creating a division between our external self and our internal self. For Rousseau, finding one's authentic self is a challenge, and society is the chief obstacle to overcoming the challenge.

Even among more properly Christian philosophers, we can detect aspects of Kennedy's idea. In his *Second Treatise on Civil Government*, the great English philosopher John Locke develops his idea of how a person can own property. His argument is that property is the just reward for labor. Our labor in the world establishes our right to own property, which we can use in what ways seem best to us.

This idea strikes many of us as entirely normal today, but it was a significant development at Locke's time. Locke argued that everyone possesses their own body, and when we labor in the world the same right to possess our bodies is extended outward to cover the things that we cultivate with our bodies. If I take the time to chop down a tree and make a chair from the wood, my right to own that chair is just as sacred as my right to control my own body. When a person labors in the world, the result of their labor is that something is transferred from the common domain (in which it belongs to the many) to the private domain, where it is the property of the laborer. At that point, "no man but he" has a right to it.[3]

In other words, if we do not have a right to dispose of our justly earned property in the way we independently choose, our bodily freedom has been violated. To be sure, Locke himself would disapprove of the lengths to which we have gone in our individualism. He actually believed that his theory of property rights furthered the *common* good by providing a way of understanding how each individual person can be provided for materially. He also condemned waste and the inordinate hoarding of wealth. Yet even so, he himself helped crack open the door to today's loneliness by giving the individual such firm control over what they may do with *their* property. By clearing the way for individual people to isolate themselves and their property from their neighbor, Locke set the stage for what followed.

We might also consider the early debates about government and politics in the newly independent United States of America. Thomas Jefferson, author of the Declaration of Independence, the nation's first ever Secretary of State, and its third president, tracked closely with the views of the French Enlightenment after spending a number of years in France as a diplomat. In one letter to his friend James Madison, he proposed that constitutions should expire every twenty-five years, at which time a new one should be ratified by the nation. Why propose something so radical and, let's be frank, unworkable? Because, Jefferson reasoned, "the earth belongs to the living."[4] A constitution that was not drafted and ratified by those currently living is, thus, an unjust infringement on their liberty. Why should their freedom to act be constrained by the beliefs of previous generations?

My point is not that each of these thinkers holds to all of the same ideas on all matters of politics or religion, nor that they are all part of some single movement advancing a single, all-encompassing agenda. History (and the people who live it) are more complex than that. Searches for grand historical conspiracies and master narratives will nearly always lead to bad historical study sooner than good practical philosophy.

The point here is not to define a comprehensive metanarrative of modern history but simply to note *one* theme that runs through a great deal of the major thinkers of the last several hundred years. What these thinkers share is a common concern with emancipating the individual from what they see to be unjust restraints on their freedom. Freedom in this understanding is an unrestrained self-expression. There are some limitations, of course—my right to self-expression does not include the right to curtail *your* right to self-expression. So it would still be wrong for me to, say, light your house on fire or hang you from a meat hook until you agree to pay me a large sum of money.

Beyond these basics, the assumption is that we have a right to self-expression, and anything which hinders self-expression is unjust. Central to this modernist story, then, is an idea that Hauerwas has elsewhere summarized this way: "I have no story except for the story I chose when I had no story."[5]

To really understand how this narrative has taken hold in the United States today, we need to consider its clearest proponents. They are a small group of mid-century French writers who called themselves existentialists. In the years after World War II, they made the case for individual freedom more effectively and clearly than anyone else had up to that point.

THE ORIGINS OF EXISTENTIALISM

If you wish to understand the modern West, you could do worse than beginning your quest in the basement of various cafés along the Left Bank of the Seine in Paris in the years after World War II. If you went there, you would find the philosophers Jean-Paul Sartre and Simone de Beauvoir holding court. From these unlikely places, Sartre and his friends crafted the philosophy that has come down to us today, in a popularized form, as the dominant idea of the modern West. Sartre and de Beauvoir were long-time lovers whose circle of romantic partners frequently included the far younger students who flocked to their tables at the cafés. For many years they were also supported in this work by the novelist and essayist Albert Camus. Though the three had their differences, there is a common thread we can discern in their various works. For each of these writers, human beings enter the world alone and independent, and they realize their identities, as it were, through action. Sartre explains it well in his essay "Existentialism Is a Humanism."

Man first of all exists, encounters himself, surges up in the world—and defines himself afterwards. If man as the existentialist sees him is not definable, it is because to begin with he is nothing. He will not be anything until later, and then he will be what he makes of himself. Thus, there is no human nature, because there is no God to have a conception of it. Man simply is.[6]

De Beauvoir—who some think was actually a more original thinker than Sartre—sums up the view even more concisely in her book *The Second Sex*, a seminal book in modern feminism. She is perhaps best known for the line that opens one of the book's sections, "One is not born, but becomes a woman."[7] What she meant should be familiar to anyone who has spent time reading about gender theory. "Woman" is a socially defined set of constructs, behaviors, and norms that one takes on, often without realizing it, as one grows up in society. It is, according to de Beauvoir, something that must be understood entirely separate from biological sex. Indeed, for de Beauvoir the good society is that which helps emancipate people from their unchosen identities, such that they can live as free human beings. This emancipation, she argues, must include emancipating us from nature itself. In a discussion of industrialization's effect on gender, she observes how it facilitated greater levels of freedom for men, and then says that women did not experience this freedom because of their ability to bear children. She writes, "In maternity woman remained closely bound to her body, like an animal."[8] Thus the existentialist story is one of liberation, of how people can be freed from unjust and unchosen norms imposed on them against their will. We might say it is the story of how the rivets, which is the word another translator used, that hold us to those roles can be removed and we can be made free.

Albert Camus develops similar ideas in his novels. He takes the abstract idea put forward by Sartre and not only personalizes it, but makes it look compelling. If, after all, there is no god, or no external, unchosen meaning given to human beings naturally, how can we experience any sort of meaning in the world? For Camus the answer is found in resisting injustice, in fighting for those who are suffering. In *The Plague*, Camus tells the story of a heroic doctor named Rieux, who puts his own life and health at risk in order to treat an outbreak of bubonic plague that strikes a city in northern Algeria near the Mediterranean coast. In Camus's gifted hands, this town becomes an analog for the world—a great evil is on the loose, indiscriminately killing. Each individual person must choose for themselves how they will respond. The heroic ones are those who choose to resist evil, even with no guarantee of success.

Indeed, Camus recognizes how hopeless all forms of resistance to evil ultimately are. As the novel ends, the plague has been beaten back in the town, though at the cost of many lives, including a close friend of Rieux. Yet even after such a great triumph, the final words are ominous:

> And, indeed, as he listened to the cries of joy rising from the town, Rieux remembered that such joy is always imperiled. He knew what those jubilant crowds did not know but could have learned from books: that the plague bacillus never dies or disappears for good; that it can lie dormant for years and years in furniture and linen chests; that it bides its time in bedrooms, cellars, trunks, and bookshelves; and that perhaps the day would come when, for the bane and the enlightening of men, it would rouse up its rats again and send them forth to die in a happy city.[9]

Though for Camus there is no hope of final triumph, there is something deeply meaningful in the act of resistance itself. In his essay "The Myth of Sisyphus," Camus wrestles with the question of morality in a world that has no predefined meaning, in which people do not have any sort of unchosen end to labor toward. Camus considers the ancient Greek story of Sisyphus, a pagan king known for his vanity. As punishment for his conceit, the king is sentenced by the gods to spend eternity rolling a boulder uphill, only to watch it roll back down the moment he steps away. Camus sees in the myth a parable for humanity. Even if there is no hope of success, we still must act. And we must do it gladly, recognizing that we can *create* a sort of meaning for ourselves through our courageous action. To borrow a popular slogan, it is not the destination that matters but the journey.

> I leave Sisyphus at the foot of the mountain! One always finds one's burden again. But Sisyphus teaches the higher fidelity that negates the

gods and raises rocks. He too concludes that all is well. This universe henceforth without a master seems to him neither sterile nor futile. Each atom of that stone, each mineral flake of that night filled mountain, in itself forms a world. The struggle itself toward the heights is enough to fill a man's heart. One must imagine Sisyphus happy.[10]

This section enjoyed a new life after the 2016 presidential elections as some young opponents of Donald Trump began using the line among themselves, saying, "one must imagine Sisyphus happy" as they described the work before them.[11] There is something many of us can relate to here, of course. The honorable defeat is a common literary trope. And even outside of Christianity, there are many people who regard martyrdom as a noble calling. Yet *honor*, as Camus defines it, remains a thin concept. As Sartre noted, there is no being outside of humanity to define what honor would be for us. And so, according to their own logic, we must define *honor* for ourselves. But once we make this move, we come uncomfortably close to the old truism that one person's hero is another person's terrorist. If we lack any sort of given standard of honor, then there isn't anything within Camus's system that closes off the possibility of a "heroic" death in service to great evil.

This raises an obvious question: If our conception of honor is little more than a projection of our own imagination into the world, how does existentialism shape our imaginations? What practices of existentialism shape our imaginations, such that we know what is honorable and what is not?

EXISTENTIALISM AND RECEPTIVENESS TO BEAUTY

To answer that question, consider the iconic carousel scene from the AMC show *Mad Men*. The scene happens in a conference room at an ad agency on Madison Avenue in New York. Ace ad man Don Draper is pitching a campaign for a new slide projector made by Kodak. The Kodak executives are in the room as Don begins. As he monologues, he clicks through photos that he has put into the projector. They are photos of his family and wife. There's an irony in all this, since by this time we are under no illusions about Don's ultimate commitment to his family—we've seen him have multiple affairs and neglect his family in seemingly every episode. Yet as he narrates, we can see that they still mean something to him. He says to the executives that their current branding for the projector—the wheel—is wrong. "This device is not a spaceship. It's a time machine." Appealing to the future is powerful, he explains, but there is an appeal to the past that can be effective as well, which we call "nostalgia." Nostalgia is difficult to use, he says, "It's delicate, but potent."

As he clicks through images of his family life, he describes the feeling powerfully, the longing we feel to get back to a place we used to love, to relive the moments whose purity and beauty linger with us even today. "It takes us to a place where we ache to go again." It's not a wheel, he says to the executives. It's a carousel, the iconic state fair ride that so many people associate closely with the innocence of childhood. "It lets us travel the way a child travels, round and around and back home again, to a place where we know we are loved."[12]

As he ponders his life, his marriage, and his children, the thing Don comes back to, the thing that actually reaches him on a deeper level, is the series of moments he shows in that presentation.

Even so, we are not unaware of how dark this view can potentially become. The hit NBC show *This Is Us* includes a particularly powerful summary of the problem midway through its first season. In it, William Hill, a man recently reunited with his long-lost biological son that he gave up for adoption as a baby, is dying from stomach cancer. In the scene, he is talking to a younger artist from New York who, somewhat insensitively, asks him what it is like to be slowly, knowingly dying. She seems to imagine it as an interesting experience, something one observes and learns from in order to inform one's art. Hill's response shatters the vanity of the artist and calls her to reckon with the severity of this freedom:

All these beautiful pieces of life are flying around me and I'm trying to catch them. When my granddaughter falls asleep in my lap I try to catch the feeling of her breathing against me. When I make my son laugh I try to catch the sound of him laughing—how it rolls up from his chest . . .

but the pieces are moving faster now and I can't catch them all. I can feel them slipping through my fingertips. And soon where there used to be my granddaughter breathing and my son laughing, there will be nothing.[13]

These scenes capture contemporary existentialism in practice. It is the person standing outside their life and clicking through still images of the past to remind themselves that life is beautiful. It is the aging person enjoying such a moment and trying desperately not to let go of it because they know they don't have many left and then . . . nothing.

We may be, in Sartre's phrase, "condemned to be free." We do not have satisfactory answers to the great questions of life—and we don't have any hope of arriving at those answers in the future. But if we attempt to live honestly, if we accept our freedom and try to use it well, we can enjoy the journey anyway because occasionally we'll experience sublime moments that make life's pain somehow worth it.

THE IMAGINATIVE APPEAL OF EXISTENTIALISM

This offer of freedom is a deeply compelling one to many people today— and for good reason. The authority structures that have traditionally told us who we can be and why have lost much of their credit in our day. Religious institutions are, as we already noted, beset by not-unfounded accusations of moral failure and gross hypocrisy. Similar claims can credibly be made about the worlds of big government and big business. The people who tell us we *can't* be free, religious leaders and their morality, parents and other authority figures and their rules, are not trustworthy. Thus the idea that their claim on us is fundamentally invalid is naturally attractive.

There is also possibility in this story. We like to be told that we can be anything we want to be, that the only limitation to what we can accomplish is our own imagination or our own willingness to put in the work to acquire a skill. It means that even if I come from limited means, I might be able "to make something of myself." Indeed, in sociologists Patrick Carr and Maria Kefalas's chronicle of life in small-town America, one of the main things they heard over and over from the more gifted high school students of small town America is that their parents and teachers regularly pressured them to leave their small town and pursue professional success in a bigger city, as if there was no life for them in their hometown.[14] This idea that I have an inherent right to be whatever I want to be is deeply American and familiar to us all. In his book *Making Sense of God*, Tim Keller notes that when the national anthem is sung at sporting events, the cheering begins on the line "o'er the land of the free." The singer quite often extends that line with a lengthy high note. "Even though the song goes on to talk about 'the brave,'" Keller writes, "this is an afterthought. Both the melody line and our culture highlight freedom as *the* main theme and value of our society."[15]

We should note one other thing about this appeal. Ultimately, the appeal can't be disproven or falsified on its own terms. The existentialist story tells us that ultimately what is wrong with the world is the fact that people do not have the freedom to be their true, authentic selves. Some good possibility for self-expression is being withheld from them, and this is the problem with the world. If people could just be free, by which we mean "if people could just have more possibilities for expressing themselves," the world would be better. So the solution to every problem is simple: more freedom. We will *always* be able to look around and find *something* that is unjustly limiting our freedom. This is why, for example, there is an inevitability to our nation's changing views on sexual ethics. What begins as an argument to be free from fixed gender roles or from unhappy marriages must then become freedom to marry a person of the same sex, which must in turn become a freedom to identify as something other than your biological sex and have the law protect your right to self-identify and perhaps even pay for any required medical treatments. Each of these movements is slightly different in one way, but they do rhyme, which is to say they share the concern with expanding a person's possible sexual identities and behaviors.

But there is a third thing we should note as we describe the emotional appeal of this story. The idea that we must picture Sisyphus happy is, in one sense, deeply empowering. If you become convinced that the act you are engaged in serves the cause of individual freedom, then you can courageously pursue that cause, even if you do not see any possibility of success. That does not matter. The permanence of whatever victory you win is likewise irrelevant. If you are engaged in the struggle to protect individual freedom, you are engaged in a worthy cause, regardless of the cause's viability or likelihood of success. Thus the call among some to resist Donald Trump's presidency by imagining Sisyphus happy.

THE PROBLEMS WITH EXISTENTIALISM

For all its imaginative appeal, which is heightened by the unique stressors of our day, the existentialist story ultimately fails. At root, an unanswerable question destabilizes the entire thing: What happens when one person's right to freedom comes into competition with another's? There may be no better illustration of the unanswerability of this question than the three French writers we have already met.

In the early 1950s, news of the gulags—Stalin's concentration camps he sent dissidents and political minorities to—was beginning to trickle out of the Soviet Union. Camus condemned the gulags in unambiguous terms, as he did all revolutionary violence. To Camus, violence was an acceptable tactic in only the most extreme circumstances, as in World War II, when he, Sartre, and de Beauvoir supported the French resistance at great personal danger to themselves. Violence executed by a state against its citizens in order to suppress political dissidents was another matter. To Camus, it represented a fundamental violation of existentialism. What greater way can there be of violating another person's freedom than coercing them via violence? Sartre, meanwhile, maintained that revolutionary violence was sometimes necessary. And so, theoretically, even something as grisly as the gulags *may* be defensible if it serves the cause of the revolution. Sartre would eventually abandon his support of the Soviet Union, but at the time of his death in 1980 he still entertained odd ideas about Maoist China, a regime that was, somehow, even more brutal than Stalin's Soviet Union.[16]

The result of this fight between Camus and Sartre was a permanent break in their friendship. De Beauvoir, predictably, took Sartre's side.

This break had dire consequences for Camus, as much of the French left went with Sartre and de Beauvoir on this question, leaving Camus as a man without a party. The right would have nothing to do with him after his early postwar activism. Now the left was against him as well. But still he held to his principles. "One must imagine Sisyphus happy." To say "this is the right thing to do, and I will do it even if it seems as absurd as Sisyphus pushing his boulder uphill" is a striking, empowering thing. The existentialist story offers that to people.

FREEDOM, LOVE, AND LIMITS

But, of course, there is a catch to all of this: it is in that word *freedom*. To be free from unjust rules or norms is good, of course, but is there more to freedom than that? If you follow the argument closely, some of the proponents of the existentialist story even acknowledge this as a problem. The left-wing philosopher Marshall Berman, whose book *The Politics of Authenticity* is a thorough argument in defense of this narrative, still cannot get away from the problem of how to maintain freedom if any forms that would shape it are unjust and immoral. He writes, "Because all persons are free and their wills are alterable, the happiness one person can give another is necessarily contingent. Certain and irrevocable possession thus defeats its own ends: the ingredient of freedom is essential to any pleasure that possession can give."[17] Later in the same chapter he writes, "Individuals must remain free to reject any system of roles which fails to fulfill their purposes, and return to anarchic freedom."[18]

What is striking about both of those excerpts is how cold they are. What has happened is that the modern story has seized on one of love's necessary qualities—freedom—and forgotten all the others. They are not wrong, of course, to note that love must be free. This is a point on which all Christians should agree. John Piper makes it well in *Desiring God* when he rhetorically asks what would happen if he brought his wife flowers, and when she thanked him, he responded by saying, "I am only doing my duty as your husband."[19] People are not projects, and the kindnesses we give to one another are not items on a checklist. On this point the existentialist story is saying something true. But freedom is not the *only* aspect of love; nor does freedom operate the same way in all relationships and situations.

In the first place, a "love" that is exclusively free and not defined by other characteristics does not change us; it does not require anything of us and does not lead to anything. The English poet W. H. Auden captured the problem well in a review of James Joyce's novel *Finnegan's Wake*. The premise here is that if individuals have a right to "reject any system of files which fails to fulfill their purposes," then we really cannot have any kind of order or structure to our loves because order itself is stultifying and repressive. But, Auden counters, "If order cannot be created, then no action can be worthwhile." If the order of marriage is inherently repressive and to be rejected, for example, then we cannot really create something larger than ourselves with our partner. As soon as we create something larger, we are no longer free. We're just short-term partners sharing resources between one another until we decide to stop doing so. Thus all that remains is to "record the flux."[20] We can try to dress that up, of course, which is precisely what Camus does with Sisyphus. Yet the fact remains that human beings strive after order and meaning that exist outside of themselves, and the existentialist story, for all the other possibilities it opens up, closes off the possibility of enduring love.

Christianity says our understanding of love comes from knowing who God is. The apostle John tells us that God is love. What does love mean, then? We can answer that question by looking at how Love himself acted in the world—love is a dying to yourself so that your beloved may live. To love another person, in this understanding, is to will their good, even at cost to yourself. To be sure, this love must still be free in the sense that it is not coerced. If I will your good but do it under duress or because of obligation, you might still benefit, but I have not shown you love, as Piper rightly says. But love must also be total, faithful, and fruitful, as Pope Paul VI helpfully summarized in "Humanae Vitae."[21] What do these three additional qualities to love mean?

When we say love is *total*, we mean that when we love another person, we do not will their good in selective ways but in its totality. If I say that I love a person, but I am acting in a way that actively harms some part of them, then I am not truly loving them. Indeed, if you will a person's good in only one area of life and ignore the others, you may end up doing real damage to them. If you will a person's professional good with no regard for any other aspect of their life, you may well encourage them toward a workaholic lifestyle *and* long-term loneliness. Similarly James warns us against pursuing a person's spiritual good apart from their physical well-being: "If one of you says to them, 'Go in peace; keep warm and well fed,' but does nothing about their physical needs, what good is it?" (James 2:16). True love wills the good of the whole person.

Love also must be faithful because when we love we do not simply will the person's good a single time and then stop. We see this in marriage and parenting, of course, but friendship should be faithful as well. In the aftermath of my father's injury, one of the qualities we most appreciated in many of my parents' friends was their fidelity. One woman from church is still mowing their yard once a week over three years after Dad's injury. We could depend on them not simply on the day of the injury but a month later, a year later, *three* years later. Yet this fidelity imposes a cost on our freedom.

The film *Secondhand Lions* captures this well. In a scene near the end of the film, a small fatherless boy who has been abandoned by his mother to be raised by his crazy great-uncles tells one of his uncles, who is prone to depression and has contemplated taking his own life, that he cannot do that because he, the small boy, needs him. "You're my uncle. I need you to stick around and be my uncle."[22] The faithfulness of love will shape—and constrain—the freedom of love.

Bonhoeffer captures this marvelously:

In the language of the Bible, freedom is not something man has for himself, but something he has for others. . . . It is not a possession, a presence, an object, . . . but a relationship and nothing else. In truth, freedom is a relationship between two persons. Being free means "being free for the other," because the other has bound me to him. Only in relationship with the other am I free.[23]

Finally, love produces fruit. We see this clearly in the love of God, which produces human beings transformed by divine grace. But we can also see it in marriage: love produces children. The fruit of a marriage is most obviously seen in the children produced by that union. We can also see it in friendship. To take one example, two friends of mine worked together to get a business off the ground, and it ended up being far more successful than they anticipated, growing into a five million dollar per year company that employs nearly forty people. That love which existed between them has helped provide a living for around a hundred people, when you factor in spouses and children of employees.

CONCLUSION

The modernist story defines *love* as that which maximizes the freedom of individual people to act and identify in whatever way they choose for themselves. This quickly leads to a problem, when one person's freedom comes into competition with another's. Because of this, love necessarily becomes a zero-sum competition in which I must maximize my own freedom even if it means undermining another person's. And so our "love" ends up being consumptive in nature—to grow itself it must cause something else to diminish. There is an image we might use to describe the erosion of community that results from this faulty story and particularly its incomplete conception of love: climate change.

Climate change is the story of how human beings have seen the chief purpose of the earth as being to facilitate their own immediate freedom from constraint, even at the cost of the planet's health. We have destroyed mountains, polluted rivers, and torn forests up by the roots, all in the quest for greater amounts of wealth and, ultimately, a life free from restraints we do not choose for ourselves. Writing about C. S. Lewis's final Chronicles of Narnia book, *The Last Battle*, Matthew Dickerson and David O'Hara argue that Lewis's villain, the old ape Shift, doesn't just treat other creatures badly (though he most certainly does that), he also symbolizes modern humanity's relationship to the physical creation.

Shift has developed an unhealthy appetite for luxuries. It is bananas and oranges (non-local food) in the first chapter, but later it becomes nuts and other foods he extorts from squirrels even though his demands may result in their starvation. The ape is prepared to manipulate the world to satisfy his lusts. He is prepared to enslave his fellow creatures and decimate the landscape, clear-cutting the trees and even starving his neighbors, to provide himself with the luxuries he desires. And Lewis makes it clear in *The Last Battle* that the consequence of this sort of behavior, if it goes unchecked, is the destruction of the earth itself.[24]

The modernist story, then, does to the social and relational climate what industrialism has done to the ecological climate. It promises great freedom but promotes it by destroying the very things that make freedom possible. So the story is inherently unsustainable and must fail, one way or another.

The story that promises us freedom if we would only have the courage to define ourselves, to create our own identities, is a cheat. It does not make us free, or rather it only makes us free by encouraging us to consume all the things that make our freedom pleasurable, to devour the things that make life lovely. In an Orwellian turn, freedom simply means a particular sort of bondage—the bondage of one's own self. We are cut off from one another because the existentialist story offers no way for us to truly approach neighbor in a posture of enduring, faithful love. We are witnesses to what happens when this idea is applied ecologically. When we do not see animals and plants and landscapes as fellow creatures to be loved and stewarded, we are alienated from them. The planet is desecrated and lives, both animal and human, are ruined or destroyed.

The spiritual outworking of this narrative is no different—the spiritual and social climates that make life beautiful are eroded by the modernist story in the same way that industrialism has eroded the physical climate. We are beginning to know this, of course. That is why we are so anxious about growing loneliness in America, the opioid crisis, and the state of our politics among other things. But we are also trying desperately *not* to know it. If we acknowledged that our ultimate understanding of personal meaning, the thing that helps us to make sense of our lives and to endure during times of pain, is purely arbitrary, the knowledge would overwhelm us. So we build walls out of stories and moments and experiences. We would rather be like Don Draper, making meaning out of the images we see click by on the carousel. But remember how that episode ends: Don doesn't come home to a full house, a warm meal, a place where he knows he is loved. His family is gone. He comes home to an empty house, darkened rooms, and silence.

FOUR

THE LOSS OF WONDER

A COUPLE YEARS AGO I was at a conference for young Christian writers located in a small town an hour north of New York City. We had broken out into smaller groups for a workshop session intended to discuss one specific question. Our group was sitting on a patio overlooking a small pond and discussing the question, What can we hope for from our life together? The group being what it was, the discussion went academic very quickly. We were debating the meaning of *liberalism*, quoting Augustine at each other, and doing all the other things nerdy young Christians do.

As we were discussing all of these things, a woman from a different discussion group brought out her nine-month-old baby son to join us. She had just finished feeding him and was now handing him off to his dad, who was part of our group. The man took his baby boy in his arms and then shifted him slightly to get him into the shade. At that point, an older woman raised her hand and asked us to stop for a moment.

"I don't want to disrupt our conversation," she said. "But I wanted us to be quiet for a moment because just now the kingdom of God came into our group—it came in the form of that little baby right there. The Bible tells us that God comes to us in unexpected ways. It tells us that he comes to us in small things. And the Gospels tell us that Jesus says the kingdom of heaven belongs to little children like that child."

Everyone's eyes shifted toward the baby. And we knew that she was right.

Some might hear that story and think it is sentimental. But in that case the joke is on them. Scripture tells us that God himself came to earth in the exact same way that small baby did. That is how God sees the world—it is something he loves and something in which the littlest things are quite often the greatest. The insides of the world are larger than their appearance would suggest. The smallest things are often the greatest. And so everywhere we look in the world there is opportunity to see something that calls us to God, the one that the Scriptures call the desire of the nations. English pastor and abolitionist John Newton, most famous for writing the hymn "Amazing Grace," understood this well. When asked how he dealt with the frustration of regular interruptions to his study as he prepared sermons, he replied, "When I hear a knock at my study door, I hear a message from God. It may be a lesson of instruction; perhaps a lesson of patience: but, since it is his message, it must be interesting."[1]

The lovely things we encounter in the world are beautiful in themselves, of course. But we should also discern something behind them—the faint echo of God's voice speaking the world into being. It's not just the thing itself we adore, whether it is the smile of a baby, the ominous sound of thunder, the beauty of a bird's song, or, if you're Newton, something as banal as a parishioner's knock on your door.

It's the shadow lingering behind that thing, just beyond our gaze. That is what we love. The great writer Italo Calvino explains it well, "You take delight not in a city's seven or seventy wonders, but in the answer it gives to a question of yours."[2] That is true of cities. It is also true of creation itself.

BORED IN THE COSMOS

In 2017 Jon Bois, a writer with the popular sports site *SB Nation*, published a short story called "17776." It was, ostensibly, a story about the future of American football. But it was so much more than that. Bois imagined a future in which an existence that sure looks like heaven turns out to be, well, kind of boring.

The story begins by explaining that a couple things happened in the early twenty-first century that changed human life forever. First, people stopped dying. No one really knew why. They just did. Second, a new kind of technology was developed that helped save people from serious injury and that could also work and grow all the food that was required for them to live. Emancipated from the need to work as well as from their own mortality, humanity now seemingly had an infinite sandbox to play in. But what if the best thing immortal and materially secure humans can do is play football?

It sounds weird at first, but Bois develops the argument well. The story is told through the lens of a few different space probes that observe humanity from outer space and enjoy rewatching classic football games when they get bored, which happens regularly. In the key section, one of the probes explains to the other why human beings never tried anything more grandiose than playing increasingly elaborate, complicated football games. Here's the answer:

> Humanity tried and tried to send themselves to other solar systems. In 3143, they succeeded, and found . . . nothing. No life. Nothing interesting. A bunch of planets full of rocks and gas. They then deployed probes to visit other stars in the Milky Way galaxy. . . . So we built what we could, and sent them out there. They found nothing even the slightest bit interesting. Everything was as we guessed it was when we saw it through the telescopes. It was the grandest anticlimax imaginable. It shattered what people thought of themselves and their destinies. The letdown was, in itself, sort of a brilliant wonder of its own. . . . People had a choice. They could continue wandering through the endless darkness, an absence of everything they loved, an endless void of disappointment and loneliness . . . or they could look down, and embrace what they always had and loved.[3]

TWO STORIES ABOUT TWO LONGINGS

Bois's story and the Christian story describe two different ways of leaning into the world. Both are playing with a common human experience. We enter the world and we encounter things in it that surprise or delight us. But the delight alone is not enough. We want there to be something more to it. We want there to be some deeper meaning that comes along with the thing itself. We want to be able to look at the world and see something greater in it. It's what T. S. Eliot has in mind when, in the *Four Quartets*, he says,

We shall not cease from exploration
And the end of all our exploring
Will be to arrive where we started
And know the place for the first time.[4]

The Christian story, which informs what that woman said about that baby, says Eliot is right. The modernist story, which Bois channels in such astonishing and moving ways, says Eliot is wrong.

In Bois's story we might imagine humanity looking at itself as it comes to terms with the opportunity it's been given: No death. No need to work. Now we can see what this world is *really* about. We can chase the desires of our hearts. The question that haunts us all is, I think, What will we find if given that opportunity?

We want to believe there is something more behind the purely physical, that the world is telling us something. Does the longing we sometimes feel tell us that there is something beyond the material world that *will* give satisfaction to that desire? Or is that desire a kind of evolutionary trick that can't be fulfilled and we must learn to ignore, if only to keep from making ourselves crazy from chasing after something that doesn't actually exist? The first story says that these whisperings we hear in the world are real and call us toward God, toward our true home. But in the second story the movement toward something grander fails. We reach all the way into space, to the stars, and we close our hand on . . . nothing.

Mad Men's Don Draper clumsily alluded to this second kind of experience, one of disappointment and questioning, when he said that "happiness is a moment before you need more happiness."[5] It's also the experience John Keats is trying to capture in his poem "Ode to a Nightingale." In it, the poet imagines himself in a wood, hearing the sound of a nightingale singing. And he hears in that sound a sort of calling, something directing his attention to a transcendent beauty that exists just beyond his grasp. So over the course of the poem, he tries various means of accessing that same world the nightingale seems to come from. First he considers wine as an entry point toward the beyond—something many people had done before Keats and many more have done since. It fails. But Keats does not stop at wine. Rather, he says, he will ascend on "the viewless wings of Poesy." If alcohol does not draw him up into this greater reality, then perhaps the beauty of art might do it. But even in the same stanza that he turns to poesy, he admits it won't work:

> But here there is no light,
> Save what from heaven is with the breezes blown
> Through verdurous glooms and winding mossy ways.[6]

Finally he turns to death itself, wondering if death might give him access to this purer realm. But even here he finds that it fails. How can he be taken up into that sense of joy and enchantment if he is not able to hear the sound that calls him to it? And so the poem ends in despair, ends with the simultaneous sense of both recognizing that something greater and more beautiful exists beyond us and yet also an awareness that we cannot access that world for ourselves. The songwriter Josh Ritter has written that "the keys to the kingdom got locked inside the kingdom."[7] That is the same idea Keats and the others are describing.

Though we may not possess Keats's poetic ability, we can still relate to him. We pass through our lives and tolerate much of the pain and sadness that comes to us because we hope it will be balanced out by something. We trust that someday a discovery will be made, a moment of bliss will find us that makes it all worthwhile, perhaps (if we are lucky) that will even explain the significance of our sadness to us. Yet we moderns in particular find ourselves far more often searching after that answer rather than finding it.

We are like the man sitting at the window in Franz Kafka's parable "A Message from the Emperor." In it a dying emperor whispers a message into the ear of his most trusted servant, a messaged that is intended for *you*: "the one apart, the wretched subject, the tiny shadow that fled far, far from the imperial sun." The emperor makes his servant repeat the message to ensure it is accurate, and then he sends him away. The servant presses through crowds and runs through hallways and out and through courtyards and then down more hallways and through more crowds, always pushing people out of his way, always pressing tirelessly forward. And yet he never seems to come closer to delivering the message. "Nobody reaches through here, least of all with a message from one who is dead. You, however, sit at your window and dream of the message when evening comes."[8]

A friend of mine talks about the experience of being a small child growing up in Manhattan and having these kinds of questions. Why can the world seem so alive with meaning one moment and so drained of it at other times? What am I seeing in those sublime moments? "When I was growing up, there were these moments in the fall when you'd be walking in Central Park, and you'd see that pink, 7 p.m.-in-September sunlight on the buildings, and it seemed like there was another place the city was pointing to."[9]

The answer that Bois suggests is the same answer put forward in different ways by Keats and by Kafka: the city isn't pointing to anything more. It does not actually offer any answers to the questions we have. There is merely the pink sunlight on the buildings. Enjoy it for what it is. But don't ask for more.

THE CHALLENGE OF DISENCHANTMENT

In his book *A Secular Age*, Canadian philosopher Charles Taylor offers an account of how the Western world shifted from the late medieval era, when Christianity touched every layer of society, to the modern era, in which even those who affirm religious belief must make a conscious belief to do so, and in which religion's influence on broader society is muted and suspect. One of the key ideas Taylor develops is that of "disenchantment." According to Taylor, the religious world of late medieval and early modern Europe was "enchanted," and the world we know today has been hollowed out, made into something base and utterly devoid of true mystery.

By now, of course, *disenchantment* is a widely discussed idea among evangelicals. Taylor has written on it extensively and is largely responsible for developing the discussion around it. Among evangelicals, James K. A. Smith, Robert Joustra, and Alissa Wilkinson have all interacted with it at length, as have a number of writers in the Gospel Coalition's 2017 volume *Our Secular Age*. Unfortunately, because *disenchantment* can mean so many things, there is much ambiguity around it.

The most literal interpretation of the idea is that we no longer believe in the supernatural. This is the just-so story you might come across from some new atheist critics and other public figures like the astronomer and TV host Neil deGraase Tyson. In this version of the disenchantment narrative, once upon a time, humans believed in angels and demons and also in faeries and wights and nyads and dryads and centaurs and satyrs. But that was before the light of modern science was shed on the world and we learned to reject such superstitious nonsense. Now we believe in science. Now we believe in observation. We do *not* believe in made-up mythical creatures. We might still believe in the teachings of a man born on December 25 who would change the world by the time he was thirty but, as Tyson trollishly pointed out on Twitter, that man is now Isaac Newton.[10]

The one problem with this convenient narrative told by more materialistic sorts is simply that it is false. Belief in the supernatural still pervades the Western world. In an extreme example, rural Romania seized the headlines in 2004 when police began arresting people for vampire slaying. (Technically they arrested them for grave desecration, but "vampire slaying" makes for better headlines.) But to the rural Romanians, their crime was trying to protect their neighbors by slaying the undead. There is even a kind of pragmatic logic to the move according to those who support the vampire slayers: "'What did we do?' pleaded Flora Marinescu, sister of the man whose body had been exhumed and the wife of the man accused of (re)killing him. 'If they're right, he was already dead. If we're right, we killed a vampire and saved their lives. . . . Is that so wrong?'"[11] Though perhaps more eye-catching, this sort of story is not uncommon in the twenty-first-century West. After all, we are only thirty years removed from the days when the Oval Office was occupied by Ronald Reagan, a man who sometimes consulted with an astrologist to help him determine his daily schedule, and whose wife would one day use mediums to try to talk to her deceased husband.[12]

This belief in the supernatural continues today. In 2017 a New York man, Adam Ellis, was in the news due to his fear that his apartment was haunted by the ghost of a small child named Dear David. Over several months Ellis documented various evidences on Twitter, using photo, video, and audio media to make the case that something wasn't right with his apartment.[13]

Alongside such anecdotes, of course, is the sheer volume of movies concerned with the paranormal that have captured attention in America and Western Europe. Certainly films like *The Exorcist* are classic examples of the genre, but then so are more recent movies like *The Witch*. Even the smash HBO hit *Game of Thrones* features wights as well as chilling supernatural creatures called White Walkers.

We also should consider polling data on belief in the supernatural. A 2005 Gallup study found that 73 percent of Americans believe in at least one of the following:

- extrasensory perception
- haunted houses
- ghosts
- telepathy
- clairvoyance
- astrology
- communicating with the dead
- witches
- reincarnation
- allowing a spirit-being to control one's body[14]

According to a 2015 Pew Research study, 29 percent of Americans claim to have communed with the dead in some way, and 18 percent claim to have seen a ghost.[15] For comparison's sake, 13 percent of Americans were receiving food stamp benefits in 2017, and roughly 15 percent of Americans have used online dating services.[16] So, statistically speaking, you are nearly twice as likely to meet someone who believes they have communed with the dead as you are to meet someone who has used Tinder or eHarmony.

When it comes to this kind of disenchantment, the meme fueled by bores like Tyson is mostly a myth. Americans *do* believe in the supernatural.

Indeed, we still believe that the world might be enchanted in some sense. Certainly we think it is filled with mysterious things we are not able to understand or adequately perceive with our senses. All that being said, while many of us have persisted in our belief in the supernatural, this belief doesn't connect to our daily life in the way that, say, belief in a sea god or fertility god connected to the life of premodern people. We still believe in the supernatural; we just don't see how it typically penetrates into our day-to-day lives, fringe cases like Dear David notwithstanding. And if we can understand how we came to think such things about the supernatural, we'll be ready to understand disenchantment properly and how it contributes to the modernist story.

THE BUFFERED SELF

You'll find a more careful use of *disenchantment* if you set aside the new atheists and read Charles Taylor and others more closely. For Taylor, whether a person believes in the supernatural or not is only tangentially related to the idea of disenchantment. Taylor is less concerned with beliefs and more with the way people experience the world. To explain how he sees the change in Western experience, Taylor speaks of what he calls a "buffered self." In an interview with the *Immanent Frame*, Taylor summarized his argument this way:

> Almost everyone can agree that one of the big differences between us and our ancestors of five hundred years ago is that they lived in an "enchanted" world, and we do not; at the very least, we live in a much less "enchanted" world. We might think of this as our having "lost" a number of beliefs and the practices which they made possible. But more, the enchanted world was one in which these forces could cross a porous boundary and shape our lives, psychic and physical. One of the big differences between us and them is that we live with a much firmer sense of the boundary between self and other. We are "buffered" selves. We have changed.[17]

Thus the persistent belief in the supernatural may complicate the general idea of disenchantment, but it doesn't actually weaken Taylor's argument because he is less concerned with belief in the supernatural and more with the experience of living in the modern West, with what our age "feels" like, as James K. A. Smith has said.[18] Indeed, Taylor's idea of the buffered self helps to explain how we can both believe in these supernatural things and, in a real sense, be mostly unbothered by them. We believe in the supernatural; we just don't think it interacts with us regularly or in a way we can control or understand. So we ignore it.

Whatever paranormal things might exist, they're unknowable, and we shouldn't bother too much about them. We believe we are closed-off individuals, self-defined and self-determined. So we believe in the supernatural in some limited way. We just don't think it affects us in ordinary circumstances.

But this belief in human individuals being closed off and sealed against the outside world has other effects as well. It doesn't just cut us off from angels and demons, it cuts us off from each other. In their book *How to Survive the Apocalypse*, Alissa Wilkinson and Robert Joustra link the idea of a buffered self to the breakdown of communal life and the many anxieties that moderns feel as they try to navigate the world.

> In the enchanted world, the most powerful location of meaning is outside of you. The very idea that there is some "clear boundary, allowing us to define an inner base area, grounded in which we can disengage from the rest," is totally absent. There isn't an essential you-ness of you; you're just a thread woven into a bigger fabric. On the other hand, modern people—you and I—tend to think of ourselves as "buffered." We are contained beings, individual agents living in a world populated by other individual agents. We have an "essential" self that is specific to us and remains us, invulnerable to outside forces (unless we let them in).[19]

Premodern people lived in a world that was mostly outside their control. If we say the world was "mysterious," we would be overstating the point—the premoderns knew far more about the world than most moderns care to admit. But with some exceptions, such as the Dutch literally claiming a country out of the swamps, much of the knowledge we had about the world simply amounted to knowledge about how helpless we were in the face of it. An agrarian existence in premodernity was frail and vulnerable precisely because it was not just a person's *identity* that depended on things almost entirely outside their control, it was the person's very life. The things that defined humans and allowed them to simply live existed outside of them and penetrated their daily life in a thousand different ways. Because of this, they experienced the world as being an enchanted place in which their own sense of self was constantly being transformed not only by other human parties but also by the mysterious, uncontrollable cosmos.

In comparison, we moderns live within parameters that we generally understand, if often in a blunt and unimaginative way, and think we control. There is very little about the world as we encounter it daily that is mysterious to us. If we encounter something we don't understand, we can pull out our phones and Google it. If there is something we don't control, it is generally something controlled by other human beings who, we assume, will behave rationally and according to discernible rules and procedures. So I may not control my employment status, but I know the person who does, and I can understand much of this person's thought about how they control my employment status. Am I doing my job well? Is the company making money from my work? These are the questions my bosses are asking, and if I know the answers, I can anticipate how they'll handle my position in the company.

Of course, relative to many in the premodern world we really *do* wield far more control over our day-to-day experience. We might say that we act on the world rather than being acted upon by the world. Farmers, to take an obvious example, are far more immune to the effects of a bad season thanks to things like fertilizer and crop insurance. Even if a season is bad, that farmer's life *can* largely go on as it did before. That wasn't the case for a subsistence farmer five hundred years ago. For these reasons, it is much easier to imagine there being a barrier between our individual self and the world around us. This creates that internal sense of the self that Wilkinson and Joustra describe, but also deprives us of something significant.

As Alan Jacobs has noted, there is a cost to disenchantment.[20] It closes us off from the demonic and affords us a more self-determined sense of ourselves, but it also cuts us off from good things as well—it cuts us off from more mystical experiences of the divine, of course, but also from the various forms of human society that exist around us and can only enter our lives to whatever extent we allow them to. Let's go back to our farmer: A combine means that he can harvest his crop quickly and easily without nasty surprises along the way. But it also means he doesn't need his children or neighbors to help with the work. Thus, there is a relationship between enchantment and communal life. Both are premised on the idea that my self is porous and can be penetrated and transformed by the world that exists outside of myself.

When we lose that sort of selfhood and replace it with the modern "buffered" self, it becomes almost inevitable that society will become more individual focused. How could it not when we see ourselves as being at our most basic level cut off from one another? This, of course, is closely related to what we saw in chapter three about the existentialist story. The disenchanted world is in many ways the environmental corollary to the existentialist story. We see humans as being at their essence—to the extent we can even speak of essences—solitary individuals, alone in the cosmos. It is unsurprising that this drift toward individualism will coincide with a weakening of communal life and the many institutions that make it possible. Thus, the work of recovering a sense of wonder in the world is intimately tied to the work of restoring the bonds of neighborliness that ought to tie us to one another.

ON BEING BORED

Other thinkers have considered this question of disenchantment as well, and though they have used different terms, their reflections are also worth considering.

In his book *Still Bored in a Culture of Entertainment*, former L'Abri worker Richard Winter tells the story of a graduate student named Mansur Zaskar, a man who attempted suicide twice before age thirty. In one meeting with his counselor, Zaskar explained himself this way:

> Most of all I feel extremely bored. Bored of everything—work, friends, hobbies, relationships, music, reading, movies, bored all the time. I do things [merely] to occupy my time, to distract myself from trying to

discover the meaning of my existence and I would gladly cease to do anything if the opportunity arose. No matter what the activity is it leaves me feeling unfulfilled. I'm bored of thinking, of talking, of feeling, bored with being bored. What possible difference does it ultimately make what I do? What difference does anything make?[21]

To be sure, some of that sounds overwrought and indulgent. You can almost picture Zaskar, dressed in all black, sitting mournfully in his room as My Chemical Romance plays in the background. But there is also something that many of us will find familiar in his bleak description of daily life. The great French Christian Blaise Pascal reckons with something like it in his *Pensées*, where he says that our condition is one of "inconstancy, boredom, and anxiety."[22]

This boredom is the more important point to consider as we discuss the idea of disenchantment. Indeed, it follows naturally from what I said earlier about the buffered self. In his book *Lost in the Cosmos*, the great Catholic writer Walker Percy observed that the root of the word *bored* is the French word *bourrer*, which means "to stuff." Think of "boring" a hole into something and you get the idea. Etymologically, the word's origins begin with calling a person "a bore," which means a person who drones on and on, almost as if they are drilling into you with their endless talk, someone who talks at you, boring into you, when you would prefer that they listen. Eventually the term *bored* grew out of that usage.

Percy asks why, exactly, human beings get bored. Animals don't get bored—they just go to sleep. And even humans don't necessarily get bored. The word *bored* comes into English in the eighteenth century, which is probably significant. As philologist Logan Pearsall Smith has said, "When anything becomes important to us it finds its name."[23] So why do modern Westerners experience this sense of aimlessness and meaninglessness in their lives? Here is Percy:

[Are Western humans bored] because there is a special sense in which for the past two or three hundred years the self has perceived itself as a leftover which cannot be accounted for by its own objective view of the world and that in spite of an ever heightened self-consciousness, increased leisure, ever more access to cultural and recreational facilities, ever more instruction on self-help, self-growth, self-enrichment, the self feels ever more imprisoned in itself—no, worse than imprisoned because a prisoner at least knows he is imprisoned and sets store by the freedom awaiting him and the world to be open, when in fact the self is not and it is not—a state of affairs which has to be called something besides imprisonment—e.g., boredom. Boredom is the self being stuffed with itself.[24]

The modern self is "buffered," meaning that there exists between us a barrier between ourselves and the world around us. Percy shrewdly cuts to the heart of the matter by noting that the issue isn't simply that we're buffered but that we're actually trapped. After all, if someone is wrapped up in a thing that isolates them from their surroundings, we would not normally call that thing merely a "buffer." We'd call it a prison. And Percy rightly notes that this is actually worse than prison because the sentence doesn't end for the bored modernist in the way it does for the incarcerated inmate. The experience of being cut off from the world, filled only with one's self, is a sentence without a release date; it is, indeed, merely the condition of one's life. Small wonder then that later in his book Percy would argue that "depression is a normal response to a deranged world."[25]

THE BUFFERED SELF AND THE NOVA EFFECT

I said earlier that the buffered self is a mostly self-defined and self-determined being, a thing which develops its own meaning and identity from the resources of its own mind and the desires of its own heart. But here we must finesse that point slightly.

Another of Taylor's ideas is the "nova effect." This is how it works: Because each of us is cut off from the world and from one another, we are free to each come up with our own quixotic approaches to the world and senses of self-identity. The result is a multiplicity of sensibilities about the world and ways of understanding it existing within a small geographic place—you might have twenty-five hundred people living within a square mile and all of them will have slightly different (or sometimes extremely different) ways of seeing themselves, ways of leaning into the world. So each of us has our own bundle of experiences, ideas, and beliefs we have molded into a personal identity, and each of us bumps up against one another every day, thereby becoming aware of other ways of leaning into the world and making sense of it.

This underscores how tenuous our own views are. We interact with hundreds or thousands of people every year who do not share our beliefs about reality. It also introduces us to new ways of understanding the self, which can be assimilated into our own sense of self. The result is that our buffered selves are also fragile and easily influenced due to the many different influences pressing in on us from all sides and attempting to shape us toward one end or another. This cross-pressure from so many different forces and angles creates a fragile identity that is always at risk of exploding in many different directions, like an exploding star, also known as a nova—thus the name.

James K. A. Smith explains it well in *How (Not) to Be Secular*:

> Sealed off from enchantment, the modern buffered self is also sealed off from significance, left to ruminate in a stew of its own ennui. It is just this sealing off that generates the pressure: the self's "relative invulnerability to anything beyond the human world" also leads to "a sense that something may be occluded in the very closure which guarantees safety." Our insulation breeds a sense of cosmic isolation.[26]

Thus, ironically, the very thing that was supposed to free people, the setting aside of religious belief and unchosen forms of identity, ends up imprisoning us. Religion, family, and place were thus not just chains but perhaps rather sources of the self, to use one of Taylor's phrases. These "limitations" formed us, made us who we are, gave us a sense of security in the world. Not only that, these things were sacramental, in the minor sense of the word—physical things we encountered in the world that gestured toward something more. Because all those things that exist outside us are now viewed with suspicion or seen as something that curtails individual freedom, we now must create all the benefits those outside sources offered from within. And we aren't able to do so.

THE POSSIBILITY OF REENCHANTMENT

Those who are bored with the world, who do not see anything in it that calls forth wonder, who look at it and see something solid all the way through, have good reason to do so. Our age pushes them toward such a sensibility at every turn. But there is another possibility. It begins with having the eyes of the woman we met at the beginning of this chapter— the ability to let ourselves see more than the simple moment in front of us. The pink sunlight on the skyscrapers *is* telling us something. The sound of birds singing at sunrise should make us think of something more. Something as small as an infant can contain worlds within itself. When we see these things and a part of us is drawn to wonder, the Christian story would have us give ourselves to that. The beauty we're seeing is real; it is not a chemical trick. And this beauty can confront us in things both large and small. Indeed, it is sometimes the smallest things that prompt the greatest astonishment. I was reminded of this several years ago while my wife was working on a farm in northwestern Iowa.

On a cool morning early that summer, I woke to the sound of my eighteen-month-old daughter, Davy Joy, babbling to herself in her crib. I went in her room, got her up, dressed her, and took her down to the kitchen for breakfast. As she ate breakfast, I grabbed a hiking backpack and set it by the door. I put her down, put on some rubber boots, and loaded her up into the pack. As I hoisted her onto my back I heard her say, "Backpack, Dada."

Before we left, I got a picture of us—both excitedly staring up into the camera, she looking every bit as eager and keen for adventure as Davy Vanauken of *A Severe Mercy*, the woman she is named after. We walked a mile and a half along a gravel road, stopping along the Soldier River to hear the sound of the water, and then continuing down the road to the farm where my wife was working in the fields. As we got closer, Davy saw her momma and, true to form, couldn't contain her excitement. She called to her from the road. I stopped, lowered her to the ground from the backpack, and she took off running just as Joie was taking off her gloves and moving toward her. Davy ran through the still-wet morning grass. A moment later her mother swept her up into her arms and hugged her.

The scene reminds me of the familiar words of the Gospel, words that the woman in our breakout session that I mentioned at the start of this chapter wanted us to remember: "Jesus said, 'Let the little children come. . . . The kingdom of heaven belongs to such as these'" (Matthew 19:14).

FIVE

THE LOSS OF GOOD WORK

Sometimes a vague desire comes to you
to own something of your own
dreaming at night
of having your own little acre of land.

MES AÏEUX, "DÉGÉNÉRATION"

"OH, YOU SHOULDN'T DO THAT." That was the response a faculty adviser offered to a friend of mine on hearing that he planned to get married in the summer after classes wrapped up. He was a junior in college. He planned to marry and then take two years to finish his undergrad degree since he was one year ahead of his fiancée. They could graduate together and then move for graduate school.

When his professor said those words, my friend asked, understandably, "Well, why not?"

"Marriage gets in the way of your work, and at this point in your career you can't afford the distraction," he responded matter-of-factly. "You absolutely shouldn't get married until you have finished your PhD. You'll be needing to write journal articles and present at conferences all through graduate school. You won't have time for a wife, let alone kids."

The advice is reminiscent of that offered by Kevin O'Leary, host of the popular TV show *Shark Tank*. When asked for advice from a young man whose fiancée had recently told him that he had to choose between running his business and their relationship, he offered a similarly blunt, calculating response: "Let's be pragmatic: Which is easier to replace? Your business or your fiancée?"[1]

In one sense, you could say both the professor and O'Leary are right: the professional world that both academics and entrepreneurs wish to enter is cutthroat. In academia, your graduate school career should be packed full not only of teaching opportunities but also research for your dissertation, additional research for submitting papers to conferences and journals, and making regular trips to events to network with others in your field as you pursue one of those rare faculty jobs after completing the program. In my friend's field, graduate work also required extensive language study. To be competitive on the market, he would need to read four or five languages fluently by the time he finished his doctorate. And even then, he'd be competing for a limited number of jobs with a significant number of recently graduated PhDs. Meanwhile in the tech world you're competing in a global market for unfathomable amounts of money and often taking very large risks. The time commitment in both cases is enormous.

Thus many young Americans now find themselves putting in enormous amounts of time at work in hopes of future success. If we want to get ahead in our careers or even just stay on track to be where we'd like to be in ten or twenty years, then we need to put in the time now. That's the myth, anyway. So we accept a lifestyle that requires us to renounce a great many of the relational pleasures that provide a sense of long-term happiness and purpose in our lives.

Writer Leah Libresco noted in an essay for *First Things* that we have a name for people who do such a thing, a name for a person who renounces many of life's ordinary pleasures to dedicate all their mental and physical resources to a singular good. We call them "monks." But today's "sad, secular monks" are quite different from their predecessors.

> A life that has no room for serious romantic partners can't have much space for deep friendships either. This should be the one culture war fight where we can all be on the same side: if careers preclude real relationships, something's gone deeply wrong. . . . If we were honest about what these jobs entail, we'd talk less in terms of success and more in terms of sacrifice and seclusion from the world. If we recognized the single-minded focus that drives Rosin's interviewees to think of intimacy

as obstacle, as life-thwarting, we might not hold it up as the ideal, the logical next step for the best and the brightest.[2]

Far from making us happy, the way we work today leaves most of us impoverished and alienated. When we combine this with the challenges posed by limitless freedom and the general malaise that haunts our nation, the results are dangerous.

THE ALIENATION OF WORK

Though we often do not experience it as such, work is supposed to be a good thing. It is one of the three things that defines human life before the fall. God places man and woman in a garden and asks them to do something. That "something" is work, and the intent was that their work would take the resources God had given them and steward them for his glory and the betterment of the place. Like God himself, we are creators who make order from what was once chaotic.

But too often our work is not a source of delight but of dread. It bores us. In many cases, it wears us down, not in the sense of making us tired— a good and normal response to hard work done well—but in the sense of eating away at us, causing us to feel as if we are being consumed, as if there will be less of ourselves left by the time we finish the job.

The consumer research organization Gallup regularly surveys workers around the world to test for what they call "employee engagement." Engaged employees are, according to Gallup, "involved in, enthusiastic about and committed to their work and workplace."[3] So how many American workers fit that description? Answer: 33 percent as of 2016. And that's actually a high mark since Gallup began tracking in 2000. Fifty-one percent of American workers, meanwhile, are disengaged.[4] The picture is even worse globally, as 87 percent of global workers are disengaged in their work according to Gallup data.[5]

How does Gallup define employee engagement? They use a methodology called the Q12—a 12-question survey given to workers. Among other things, it asks if employees have "the opportunity to do what you do best every day," and "does your supervisor, or someone at work, seem to care about you as a person?"[6] The sad, though unsurprising, reality of our day is that most Americans do not find their work satisfying and do not even have a person at their place of employment who cares about them as an individual.

Why are we so disengaged? Well, the story that opens this chapter provides one answer. For many Americans, the way we work is deeply draining and alienating. As Libresco noted, most careers are not really *vocations* in the purest sense of the term. A vocation is a calling, ultimately something that God calls us to do or pursue. We all share one common vocation in that we are all made to know God. But then we are also uniquely gifted in various ways. Thus we have distinct vocations as well that are used to help others be drawn into the good life of happiness and bliss in knowing God and loving the people and things God has made.

While we should always aspire to professions that serve people in some way, most of us will not find complete vocational fulfillment in our work. We might be called to marriage and parenting or to a life among the poor in our community or perhaps to running a ministry that assists youth in our church or city. These are all worthy callings, but in most cases they will not be professions.

Yet when our professions demand so much of us that they crowd out these other things, we find ourselves feeling simultaneously busy and disillusioned. We pursue a line of work, pour so much of ourselves into it, and yet many of our desires and longings in our lives, in our work, are left unfulfilled. This happens because our professions end up consuming an outsized portion of our lives and leave little room for anything else, including intimacy and friendship.

One wealthy Silicon Valley resident captured the problem neatly—and quite unintentionally—as she relayed a conversation she had with her father: "I was talking to my father on Skype the other day. He asked, 'Don't you miss a casual stroll to the shop?' [I said,] everything we do now is time-limited, and you do everything with intention. There's not time to stroll anywhere."[7]

If there is no time for a stroll to the shop, I can't help wondering what there *is* time for. And it's not only the rich that are affected by this either.

As wages stagnate, benefits diminish, and jobs disappear, many Americans are being forced to take additional side-hustle jobs to help pad their meager savings or, more likely, to make ends meet. These jobs, part of the so-called gig economy, can range from driving for ride-sharing services like Uber or Lyft to making deliveries for grocery or restaurant delivery apps to cleaning homes or apartments with yet another app. These workers are never classified as employees but as independent contractors, which means their wages are not regulated in the same way by minimum-wage laws, and they do not receive benefits.

In a story for the *New Yorker*, Jia Tolentino describes how this economy is really the perfect symbol for the way our current economy is quite willing to extract every bit of value it can from the less wealthy before shunting them aside like used parts. Tolentino cites as an example an ad for the online service marketplace Fiverr, which features a bleary-eyed woman coolly staring into a camera with the caption reading, "You eat a coffee for lunch. You follow through on your follow through. Sleep deprivation is your drug of choice. You might be a doer." Tolentino argues that, far from being a thing worth celebrating, the gig economy is actually one of the clearest pictures of how the American system encourages or even forces people to give up everything else that makes life worthwhile in the service of the almighty dollar:

> At the root of this is the American obsession with self-reliance, which makes it more acceptable to applaud an individual for working himself to death than to argue that an individual working himself to death is evidence of a flawed economic system. The contrast between the gig economy's rhetoric (everyone is always connecting, having fun, and killing it!) and the conditions that allow it to exist (a lack of dependable employment that pays a living wage) makes this kink in our thinking especially clear.[8]

Whether we are making a great deal of money or simply scraping by while working obscene hours, the way we work today crowds out a great deal of life. It consumes us and leaves little space for family or friendship or even simple recreation. We're all simply too busy. One obvious question, then, is how we came to work so much only to receive so little.

THE HOLLOWING OUT OF WORK

In the 1970s the US Secretary of Agriculture was Earl Butz. Under Butz's oversight, American agriculture underwent a radical transformation as it became oriented chiefly toward profitability and began to mirror the kind of work that is valued in offices and on Wall Street. Butz's chief goal was to make the American agricultural system more efficient according to the standards of the market. For Butz, wealth is not about land and work; it is about money and industry. His two mottoes were "get big or get out" and "adapt or die."

This likely tells you all you need to know about the man.

If there were two ways of doing the same task and one way required ten people to do and the other required two, it was self-evident to Butz that the latter was preferable. Most of America agreed with his judgment, which is why the share of the population living on farms and in rural America continued to drop throughout the 1970s, a trend that has largely continued to the present day. There were, however, some dissenters.

The most well-known dissenter is likely the Kentucky writer Wendell Berry. In a debate with Butz, Berry raised what he saw as the chief problem with the secretary's understanding of farming. Butz, said Berry, is concerned only with efficiency. But efficiency is only one way of understanding and judging work. After all, there are many ways we might both make our lives more efficient and much worse. Taking the time to read my children a story before putting them to bed is not necessarily efficient, but it is good. To judge something like parenting on the basis of efficiency is simply a category error. But what if that is true of *most* work human beings do? What if there are higher goods than machine-like efficiency?

This is the concern Berry raises in responding to Butz: it might be more efficient for farms to run like modern industrial enterprises, but it would also make them much less like farms. To farm well you must embrace many values that are not themselves efficient—an attentiveness to the land, a concern for what it needs and not what can be extracted from it, and a general understanding that, as Berry puts it in one of his novels, the farm will outlive the farmer and so the farm's needs should be given primacy. A farm is more a creature than a machine. To treat it as if it is the latter is a mistake. More than that it is a mistake that can hurt not only the farm but the people who draw their life from the farm—which is to say everyone.

In the debate Berry says that while Butz is concerned with efficiency, he is concerned with values. Specifically he is concerned about the effect that a single-minded focus on efficiency will have on the values of rural places in particular and on America more generally. The way Berry makes the point is important: the issue is not that efficiency and a concern with profitability are, in themselves, destructive of the virtues Berry cherishes. Profitability can be a great good. Indeed, in an industrial economy profitability is essential for the ongoing existence of businesses, which serve as one of the chief forms of community for many people in an urban society.

That said, when efficiency and profitability become the only thing, they pervert everything they touch. They become a danger to those virtues because they are a danger to the people who embody those virtues and pass them on to future generations. "How can we have traditional values," Berry asks, "if we don't have the traditional people who embrace those values?"[9] And how, we should add, can we have traditional people if we are indifferent to the places and institutions that produced and sustained those people?

Butz's system made sense on paper, in other words, but it was a suicide machine. It needs responsible, conscientious human beings who do good work to run it, the sort who can recognize when an added efficiency would improve the work and who can also recognize when greater efficiency would actually hurt the work. However, it simultaneously destroys the communities that produce those kinds of human beings. This then is the material problem of our day: Healthy human societies run on a certain kind of human fuel, we might say. Any society that is to be healthy and sustainable in the long run, then, must not only produce enough material wealth to provide for its physical existence, it must also produce the kind of people who can create that wealth and pass on the virtues that allow them to do so to future generations.

The problem we face today is that Butz's view of work has won—and not just in agriculture. It has won everywhere. And the result is that work has been hollowed out, transformed, and far removed from its original meaning.

What is the original meaning of work? I will say more about this in chapter eight but I can say this for now: in the creation account of Genesis 1–2, work is something God gives Adam and Eve to do as they cultivate the garden he has put them in. Note carefully the specific sort of work God gives the first man and woman. It is work within a garden, their home place in the world, and work that is meant to not only bring further order to the creation but to make it more fruitful. The command given to Adam and Eve to be fruitful and multiply—obviously a command associated with child-bearing—is linked in the same sentence with "having dominion" over the world.

But the idea of "dominion" here is not a kind of mindless control or exploitation. Rather, it is to take something that exists and is already good and to make it better, so that the world more closely resembles the intentions of God and is able to more richly bless our neighbors. Thus one of the key aspects of work in this text is not simply *what* is being done but *where* it is being done and *who* it is being done for. Good work does not simply yield a material surplus, though it does that. It also serves the health of a place by ordering its life to look more the way God wants it to look. And it dignifies the individual by giving them a part to play in turning the creation toward God's ends. The divide between home, small communities, and work is blurry in the Genesis account, to the extent that it exists at all. Thus one way of understanding the tragedy of our current economy is in noting how far apart home, community, and work have become.

This process, which began with the industrial revolution, as home ceased to be productive in itself, is described by Nancy Pearcey in her book *Total Truth*.

> The [preindustrial] pattern was based on *personal* relations between a farmer and his sons and hired hands, or between craftsman and apprentices. In the Industrial Revolution, that gave way to *impersonal* relations based on wages. . . . The new workplace fostered an economic philosophy of atomistic

individualism, as workers were treated as so many interchangeable units to be plugged into the production process—each struggling to advance himself at the expense of others. To many, the world of industry seemed to be a Social Darwinist war of each against all. (Some have even suggested that Darwin's concept of the struggle for existence was merely an extrapolation into biology of the competitive ethos of early industrialism.)[10]

In a preindustrial setting—or at least a functioning, healthy preindustrial setting—the divide between work that provides for one's material existence and work that strengthens bonds of family and friendship through cooperation and shared place was largely nonexistent. Work, by both mother and father, was done in the home. True, there was still a divide in the work as much of the preparation of meals, cleaning, and maintaining of the home itself fell to women, and the care of the land and work that brought in an income typically fell to men. But in this model the divide is less important than the unifying theme of a shared place with a shared end—the provisioning of the family. Put another way, the older model explicitly tied "work" to what Presbyterian pastor Christopher Wiley calls "an economy of love." My work was quite obviously tied to my family's welfare, and so I could easily discern how my work served them. Thus I was able to offer that work up to them (and to God) as a gift of love. Wiley explains the idea well: "Productive property gives the household economy something to work on together, something to offer the world in exchange for a living."[11] What happens when this is removed? Wiley, again, is helpful:

> Something is happening today that is impoverishing us, even as we are growing wealthier than ever: we're cashing in the household economy. More than ever people work outside the home, exchanging love for money. The household economy is broken. Husbands and wives now have separate careers, separate bank accounts, separate names, and in some cases, even separate vacations. But the household economy is based on giving. It's emotionally rich and densely meaningful because it is an economy of love. The closest thing we have to it is the economy of God.[12]

The result of this transformation, of course, is that the home is hollowed out. Once a place of productivity and meaningful work, it has become a storage facility and consumption hub. The work of a stay-at-home parent, then, is reduced to the coordination of consumption and maintenance of a storage facility. It is, in other words, identical to the work required by many jobs offered outside the home which, if nothing else, at least offer the benefit of a paycheck.

We should not be surprised, then, that the work of the home has become tedious to both men and women. It is hard to be enthused for unpaid labor that produces nothing concrete. It was only a matter of time before men and women alike would flee the home, embracing the capitalist marketplace as the only place where their calling as workers can be fulfilled.

WORK'S DISTANCE FROM HOME

This distance between work and home should also be understood in more concrete terms. It is not just that our work is removed from home in a metaphorical sense but that our work is often quite literally a long distance from our homes. When I had recently graduated from college, I moved to a large Midwestern city and joined a church where I already knew a number of people, including the senior pastor. I joined a small group and started going every week. Unfortunately, the group was composed of people from many different phases of life, with different schedules, and living all across the metro area, which consisted of nearly four million people. Some people had to drive an hour round trip just to get to small group. Others had kids in school who needed to be home and in bed at an early hour. And still others worked late, and, when combined with their commute time, could only arrive shortly before other people had to leave. The result was that we had a very small window in which to share prayer requests, discuss the book or portion of Scripture we had read that week, and converse and get to know one another.

Unsurprisingly, it was hard to develop a strong connection to the other people in the group. Some of us managed it in time, but it was difficult, and some people inevitably couldn't make it work and fell out of the group. There simply wasn't enough time in the evening to get to know one another. And scheduling times to hang out during the rest of the week? It could be done with enough planning, but it wasn't easy, and even then it probably only happened once every four to six weeks.

This is a common problem for many people, of course. Professionals work jobs that may be forty hours a week on paper, but in practice the actual time on the clock is often north of fifty or fifty-five hours. Add in commute times, and "work" may end up consuming half the hours of our day. Family often takes up the remainder of that time, especially for parents with children who need to be in bed early or who have youth sports, music lessons, or some other extracurricular activity.

On this admittedly simple analysis, there simply aren't enough hours in the day to leave room for coffee with friends, serving in local voluntary organizations, or having a recreational habit that helps us develop relationships with neighbors or peers. It's all we can handle to work a full-time job and maintain some semblance of family life.

Singles and young professionals are often not much better off than the families. Though they do not have parenting responsibilities to claim their time, they are often locked into even more rigid work schedules, either because they are putting in long hours to try to get ahead early in their careers or because they are working two or three jobs just to get by and pay the bills and, most likely, service whatever loan debt they took on in order to pay for college.

Viewed this way, you might say that community is a math problem where the numbers do not add up: it requires a certain amount of openness in our schedule to allow for time with others, and most of us simply don't have the room and don't see any way to make it. If we assume that around sixty hours of our week is spent at work or commuting to and from work—a conservative estimate in many places, particularly in upwardly mobile coastal cities with bad commutes—and that fifty hours is spent on sleep (which would equate to seven hours a night, which is the minimal amount most doctors recommend), well, that doesn't leave a lot of time for community life. After all, with those remaining hours we need to make meals, shop for groceries, clean house, spend time with a spouse or kids (if married), possibly take kids to youth sports events or other extracurriculars, and so on. There simply isn't much room for unhurried time—and that sort of time is often what allows us to form thick relational connections with other people.

Worryingly, this fast-paced life is becoming more the norm, especially in major coastal cities where the high cost of living forces many workers to live long distances from the city. There is a new phenomenon beginning to emerge around "extreme commuters." In one case, the *New York Times* interviewed a man who explained that he never saw his son during the week due to his four-hour round-trip daily commute, but it was worth it because the commute allowed him and his wife to afford a larger home on a bit of land out in the country.[13] In such a situation, a person is basically making a choice to have their entire communal life exist around the workplace, which is to say their entire communal life exists around a fragile community whose whole existence depends on the profitability of the enterprise and good will of the employer.

THE PERVERSION OF WORK

Given these many changes in the nature of work, two things had to happen: first, a sociological shift, and, second, an economic one.

First, as a result of our alienation from home, family, friends, and religious life, jobs and professions have had to take on a greater emotional significance. The job is not only a place to earn an income. It is taking on roles traditionally associated with a home. So the paycheck alone is not the point, really. The significance found in the home has to be found somewhere. And where else would such significance be found, given what had been done to the home?

Moreover, as knowledge work grows more common and manual labor and the trades are sidelined, the problem becomes sharper due to the nature of the work. When an electrician wires something incorrectly, the error is obvious and, significantly, constrained to his actions in a single moment. There is no necessary commentary on his value as a person in the failure; he simply made a mistake. The mistake can still be dangerous, of course, which is why it matters. But correcting the mistake is also not difficult. With knowledge jobs, the work is of a different sort. Failures are not as apparent; nor are the objective standards that could be used to judge a person's work. As Matthew Crawford writes, "American businesses have shifted their focus . . . to the projection of brands, that is, states of mind in the consumer, and this shift finds its correlate in the production of mentalities in workers. . . . In the contemporary office, the whole person is at issue, rather than a narrow set of competencies."[14]

As a result of the increased emotional significance we attach to work in the marketplace, even households that do not require both spouses to work will often maintain two incomes because one or both partners feels as if their life would lack significance without the benefit of conventional salaried work in the capitalist marketplace. One of the ways our economy impoverishes us spiritually is by teaching us that the only sort of work that is *really* work is work that a member of the capitalist class will pay us to do in the form of a wage of some sort. But there is plenty of good work to be done in our neighborhoods and cities that the market does not recognize. Indeed, as the American home is further eroded, there is plenty of work that desperately needs to be done but will not be recompensed by a member of the capitalist class. Who will create places of warmth and safety for children to come home to? Who will provide help with childcare during the day so a young parent can run a few errands? Who will visit the elderly shut-in whose family lives several hours away? Who will spend an hour reading with a child so they can grow up knowing the delight of stories and books?

One refreshing exception to this rule is a family we know from a nearby church. The wife has a well-paying job that is able to cover the family's needs. This frees up the husband to use his time to do other forms of work that the marketplace does not value but are nonetheless useful to our city. He serves as a volunteer referee in youth soccer, serves on multiple neighborhood and local service-oriented boards, and runs a food distribution ministry out of his church, which provides free food to low-income families. None of these jobs pay a competitive market salary, but all are forms of work that serve the well-being of his place. But when we treat "work" and "a job in the marketplace" as being synonymous, the opportunities to do this sort of work end up disappearing before we can even look for them.

This brings us to the second, economic problem. As explained in books like Thomas Piketty's *Capital*, we live in a world in which the returns made by the owners of productive property—be that rental properties, businesses, intellectual property, stocks, or some other sort of capital—grow at a much faster rate than wages are growing. The result is the creation of a two-class society with the property owners riding high and the workers languishing behind.

Though the rich have gotten *dramatically* richer in the past fifty years, wages have stagnated even as the cost of living has increased. Adjusted for inflation, the average hourly wage in 1964 for a typical American worker was $19.18 an hour. In 2014 the average wage was $20.67.[15] Given the increases in the cost of housing and medical care especially, to say nothing of the massive growth in student loan debt, those basically identical wages do not cover nearly as much in 2014 as they did in 1964.

One might argue that income inequality is not a problem as long as the underclass has enough to live comfortably, but as the cost of living in the United States continues to go up, more and more Americans do *not* have enough to live comfortably. According to a 2014 *New York Times* report, 51 million Americans earn less than 50 percent above the poverty line, which, by one measure, places them in a category called "near poor." Of these 51 million, 28 percent work full-time jobs but do not earn enough to clear the "near poor" threshold. Moreover, a quarter of these 51 million do not have health insurance—a luxury they are not able to afford, even after the Affordable Care Act's passing in 2010. When we combine this group with the number of Americans who *are* living below the poverty line, the results are sobering: one in three Americans either are living at the poverty level or in "near poverty," which is to say they're essentially living paycheck to paycheck with little to no savings.[16] This, of course, is why we are seeing the rise of side hustles and the gig economy.

Theoretically, set-your-own-hours jobs with services like Uber should offer wages that can help supplement what is lacking from other employment. Yet the very nature of the gig economy exacerbates the problem. True, it allows workers who need money to pick up some extra cash on the side. But the vast share of the wealth produced by these new apps and sharing services still ends up going to the economic elites—to venture capitalists who invest in the companies and to the usually well-off founders who launch the businesses. This is how we end up in a nation where Amazon's chief executive, Jeff Bezos, will quite literally make millions before he finishes breakfast, while other Americans won't even have clean water or enough food.

WHO OWNS THE PRODUCT OF MY WORK?

Fixing these problems will require dramatic action by many different parties. Business owners will need to take steps to increase wages while the government will likely need to find ways of addressing some of the largest costs that the average American faces—most notably the costs of higher education and medical care. But generally speaking, neither of these things are happening; wages are not going up and the government is unable to act. Why?

One of the underlying assumptions we bring into discussions of work today is that a person has an absolute right to dispose of their personal property in whatever way seems best to them. This is why many Americans get nervous, for example, when we suggest that the rich should be taxed at a higher rate in order to finance a stronger social safety net. We tolerate some level of taxing to provide for these needs, but though most of us are not libertarians who condemn taxation as a form of government-sanctioned theft, there is still a certain discomfort here: how much of that person's money should be taken to provide for a valuable public service? Our underlying principle is that if we own it, we can do what we want with it. If government or anyone else wants to *tell* us what to do with it, this would be an exception to the rule, and they'd best have a *very* good reason for taking away our liberty in this way. But the idea of personal property, so obvious and intuitive to us today, is actually quite new, historically speaking.

The key figure to understand in the development of this idea is the English political philosopher John Locke. Locke introduced a new idea about property, specifically the idea that I can have an absolute claim on "my" property.

I mentioned this briefly in a previous chapter. Locke's notion of work, however, is key to understanding this transformation. As I noted, for Locke once a person produces something through their bodily labor, their ownership of that product is as certain as their ownership of their own body. By isolating the fruit of a person's work from the people the work is done for and the place where the work is done, work's product ceases to be a holistic human good and becomes a purely monetary good.

Before Locke, the belief among most Western Christians was that ultimately the world and everything in it belonged to God. For practical reasons, people were free to define property rights legally as a way of stewarding resources more effectively. God may own it all, but someone has to be responsible for how a resource is used. So the government could say that property x belonged to person y and was theirs to steward in service of the common good. But the notion that anyone "owned" property in the sense Locke meant was not typical. In a paper written for the *Journal of Markets & Morality*, Richard Dougherty explains the pre-Lockean understanding of property in two famous doctors of the church, Augustine and Thomas Aquinas.[17] In both cases, we find that their understanding of property rights looks quite different from Locke's.

Thomas Aquinas, for example, noted that there are limits as to how we can use our property. In considering the Old Testament law, Thomas notes that there are a number of lessons in those texts for how we should think about property today. In Numbers 33 when the land of Canaan was divided up for the possession of the Israelites, there were three provisions introduced to limit how much land a person could own and what they could do with it.

First, the land was distributed equitably across all the people.

Second, the law made it impossible for anyone to lose their familial land permanently. Every fifty years Israel was to celebrate the Year of Jubilee. As part of the celebrations, debts were forgiven and land was returned to the family who first owned it.

Third, the law required that land be passed down through families, and in the event of only female heirs, the heiress could marry only within her tribe, thereby guaranteeing that the land stayed with the specific tribe it was given to.

Further, Thomas noted that the law made additional provisions that complicate what we mean by a person "owning" their property. The command to leave behind crops that were dropped during harvesting highlights the fact that in one sense the poor have a right to the produce of the land as well. We see this in the book of Ruth, of course, when Ruth gleans from the field of Boaz to provide for food for herself and Naomi. Additionally, during the Sabbath years, anything grown from the land, which was not to be worked that year, was held in common among all God's people. In all these ways, Christianity tells us that while there is a limited sense in which a person can own property, that ownership is conditional.

The tendency these norms around property worked toward was also quite easy to anticipate: the goal was love of neighbor. Thomas put it well, "All the precepts of the Law, chiefly those concerning our neighbor, seem to aim at the end that men should love one another."[18]

The early Protestant Reformers were also less modern on these matters than most people realize. Commenting on Isaiah 58 the French Reformer John Calvin wrote:

> By commanding them to "break bread to the hungry" he intended to take away every excuse from covetous and greedy men, who allege that they have a right to keep possession of that which is their own. "This is mine, and therefore I may keep it for myself. Why should I make common property of that which God has given me?" He replies, "It is indeed yours, but on this condition, that you share it with the hungry and thirsty, not that you eat it yourself alone. And indeed this is the dictate of common sense, that the hungry are deprived of their just right if their hunger is not relieved. That sad spectacle extorts compassion even from the cruel and barbarous."[19]

In other words, for Calvin the right to property is conditional, and the condition is that we share our property with those who have need. To be sure, the early Protestants taught that people should seek to make as much money as they can, but the whole point of doing that was precisely so they could give away the vast majority of it. Theologian Matthew Tuininga made the point: "The Christian tradition has unanimously affirmed that all property rights are always qualified by the claims of the needy upon them."[20]

To be sure, Locke himself tried to build in safeguards to protect his ideas from being abused. That said, by giving the owner of property an absolute claim on the property obtained through their labor, he opened the door for others to follow after him and remove more and more of the safeguards that Locke attached to his dangerous idea. The result is the social order we have today, where many American Republicans and, indeed, many American evangelicals, see no problem with the fact that millions of Americans cannot afford adequate health coverage and struggle to find enough food to feed their families.

Even now, however, there are Christians who are clear about the evil of this economy, and we would do well to heed their words. In *Evangelii Gaudium*, Pope Francis has written:

> Solidarity is a spontaneous reaction by those who recognize that the social function of property and the universal destination of goods are realities which come before private property. The private ownership of goods is justified by the need to protect and increase them, so that they can better serve the common good; for this reason, solidarity must be lived as the decision to restore to the poor what belongs to them.[21]

In other words, our physical property and the physical world itself are not objects to be owned and consumed in whatever way the owner of the property deems fit. They are to be stewarded for the good of all people, and when we fail to do this we are, according to Christianity, engaging in theft, which is, of course, a violation of the Eighth Commandment.

FREEDOM AND ECONOMICS

Such an idea, of course, is practically unimaginable to many, particularly to political conservatives. In their view, attaching such conditions to the right to own property is an intolerable curtailment of individual freedom.

This is how the economist Milton Friedman, a notable free-market theorist, made the point: "[A free-market economy] gives people what they want instead of what a particular group thinks they ought to want. Underlying most arguments against the free market is a lack of belief in freedom itself."[22]

Friedman is presenting the economic version of Justice Kennedy's words cited earlier: "Essential to the idea of freedom is the right to define one's own concept of existence." If a group attempts to tell me, the private consumer, what I should or should not want, that group is violating my freedom.

This may be a common idea, but it is not remotely a Christian one. Christianity tells us that the greatest good a human being can experience is to fulfill the Great Commandment, which is to love God and neighbor. The way we show this love is known to most Christians: We evangelize, engage in acts of mercy, worship as a church body, and so on. In the ordinary course of discipleship, we routinely shape the desires of people. In Friedman's terms, we are a group of people who routinely tell other people what they ought to want. This is because we believe that Jesus is God, that he came from the Father, that he was crucified, buried, rose from the grave, and one day will return to judge the living and the dead. Because these things are true, Christians call the whole world to respond rightly to his news, to repent and follow Christ. In proclaiming the gospel we are telling the world what it ought to desire—Christ above all, but then a number of other secondary goods as well.

Friedman's assertion is that whatever we think of religion and church, those ideas should not be translated into our economic lives unless we choose to take those beliefs into our economic lives as private individuals. But for Friedman's economic theory, whether I choose to want a quiet home with family and close friends nearby or I wish to become the "Wolf of Wall Street" is immaterial. We might make private moral judgments about what a person should want, but no group has the right to tell an individual what to do with their wealth. If you have the money to purchase a thing and there's a seller out there willing to offer it, then you should be able to buy it, no matter what some other group of people might think. It's your property, after all.

That being said, we should consider what happens in a world where each individual is free to steward their physical means to obtain whatever end they themselves choose to pursue. If there is no common good that all people are unified around and wish to pursue collectively, then there is no shared thing that people are trying to take hold of and enjoy together. There is only a bundle of competing private goods each individual wants for themselves. In the quest to obtain those goods, these people will compete with each other. Indeed, the market economy expects them to. What happens then? Theologian William Cavanaugh explains,

> The absence of objective goods does not free the individual, but leaves him or her subject to the arbitrary competition of wills. In other words, in the absence of a substantive account of the good, all that remains is sheer arbitrary power, one will against another. . . . Without the idea that some goods are objectively better than others, the movement of the will can only be arbitrary.[23]

This, of course, is precisely what we find when we look at today's economy. Over 150 years of industrialized capitalism, wealth, and power has gradually been concentrated in an ever smaller share of the population, with the result being that a small number of people exert an historically unfathomable amount of power over the day-to-day lives of people—down to being able to monitor how fast an employee walks on the factory floor, for example. In our economy today the only good we wish to pursue is cheaper goods, which we obtain through the mistreatment or outright elimination of workers.

We have created a kind of invisible force field around the market in which morality is allowed to penetrate only occasionally and only on the terms that "the market" (by which I mean the owners of productive property) allows. Certainly most of us would still hold that it is better to be kind and honest in one's work, although that frequently does not seem to apply to many otherwise very successful business people. But even there, we are reluctant to mount moral critiques of the market economy itself. We will grant that it is better if people working *within* that system are decent moral people.

But to question the basic integrity of industrial capitalism is a step too far for many evangelicals, though thankfully there are writers like Pearcey and Wiley who recognize the underlying issues. Most of us, of course, are comfortable saying that a manager at Walmart should speak kindly to their employees. We care a great deal about manners, after all. But are we prepared to say that the same manager should do what they can to advocate for a living wage for their employees? Are we prepared to say that the C-suite executive at Walmart should make decisions based not only on the business's ledger but also on what is best for the communities where their stores are located? Far too often the answer is no, and so a large portion of our lives and one of the most decisive factors influencing the sort of neighborhoods, cities, and even nation that we will have is allowed to exist in its own silo, cut off from the plain truths about human beings taught in Scripture.

CONCLUSION

We have already seen that individuals in our society have good reason to be anxious and discontent. We have also seen that our modern ways of thinking about work provide no real incentive to do anything about that anxiety and discontent.

The result is that many of the things that make life enjoyable and beautiful become practical impossibilities for many people, or at least more difficult to obtain than they ought to be. A mother cannot enjoy time with her newborn because she has to go back to work almost immediately after having the child. A lonely twenty-something struggles through life in a new city where she doesn't know anyone and doesn't have time to develop relationships outside of the office, which is pressure-packed because it is her first job and she's keen to impress her boss. Children grow up never knowing their grandparents because they live in another state and only see each other a few times a year. A senior citizen is exiled to a retirement home not because of unique medical needs that would merit such care but simply because he has no one to take care of him.

All these various signs of communal breakdown still benefit *someone*. The mother of the newborn who has to go back to work benefits her employer. The lonely twenty-something benefits her employer and her creditor who paid for her undergrad education and is now getting paid back with interest. Public schools and daycare owners benefit from children estranged from their families because they can now receive funds to provide additional care for that child. And the aging senior citizen? Large nursing homes will happily collect rent and a number of other fees in exchange for caring for that person in their old age. When the market consumes traditional communities, it is happy to turn around and produce pale imitations of them.

In a song called "Dégénération," the Quebec band Mes Aïeux described the generational decline seen in twentieth-century Quebec. The song reflects on the change that happens in four generations—a great grandfather clears the land and begins to farm it. The grandfather establishes it as a profitable farm. The father sells it for a fortune. And the son? He moves to a city and chases odd jobs he can find from a studio apartment he can barely afford. That decline, "degeneration" in the pun title of the song, is what we have described so far. It is a bleak picture, moving from hopefulness and agency in the past to despair and isolation in the present.

But it does not need to be the end of the story. Though we have grown estranged from one another, bored with the world, and frustrated in our labor, we need not stay in this place. There is a still more excellent way of being in God's world than what we have seen as we consider our present condition in America.

PART THREE

THE
PRACTICES
OF
COMMUNITY

SO FAR I HAVE SKETCHED A BLEAK PICTURE of the contemporary United States both in the sphere of religion and common life more generally. I have also outlined the reasons for our national malaise, which concerns the felt loss of meaning, wonder, and the absence of good, sustainable work.

Now I turn to hope. In the face of such darkness, what legitimate grounds do we have for hope? There are two sources: first, human creatures must hope because they themselves are proof of the abundant, overflowing life of the transcendent God. In our embodied life in a physical world we are a constant reminder of the life of the God who was perfectly complete and content in himself and created out of that abundance. Our Creator is filled to the brim with joy. One day we will be too. That's the long-term reason for hope.

The short-term reason is the simple fact that each of us maintains some level of agency in the world. There is some space available to us in life that we can shape according to conviction and out of a desire to keep faith with all that is good and lovely in this world. Wendell Berry has said that if a person can require something of themselves and then maintain that practice, they have grounds for hope.[1]

Thus the most important political action Christians can engage in is simply practicing ordinary Christian piety—practicing the sabbath, making ourselves at home in the world, and, as much as possible, giving ourselves to good work. Our work in particular can take many forms, of course. One person is called to work as an electrician, another works as an accountant, and still another is an entrepreneur. Some of us will be called to politics. Work is simply the way human beings offer their abilities and time back to God in service of neighbor.

This is the stuff on which communities are built or reinvigorated. It's also roughly what God tells his people to do through the prophet Jeremiah in Jeremiah 29. When instructing them as to how they should live while in exile in Babylon, God gives his people very basic instructions:

> Build houses and settle down; plant gardens and eat what they produce. Marry and have sons and daughters; find wives for your sons and give your daughters in marriage, so that they too may have sons and daughters. Increase in number there; do not decrease. Also, seek the peace and prosperity of the city to which I have carried you into exile. Pray to the Lord for it, because if it prospers, you too will prosper. (Jeremiah 29:5-7)

What evangelicals most need to do in the political arena today is not elect certain candidates or support certain legislative causes. There is a place for that, to be sure. But the most important thing we can do is be properly Christian in the totality of our lives, starting with the way we shape our homes and carrying that out into our individual vocations, whatever those may be.

Where do those sorts of Christians come from? That is the question we will turn to in part three. The short answer is that faithful Christians are the natural fruit of patient faith in God and cultivation of Christian virtue over time. Eugene Peterson memorably used the phrase "a long obedience in the same direction" to describe this process. Specifically, our long obedience consists of a few simple practices that can be seen clearly in Scripture. In the creation account of Genesis 1–2 the text describes three things that are good, normal parts of human life prior to the fall and the invasion of sin into God's good world. Those three norms are work, home, and sabbath. The simplest place to begin in recovering common life is in recovering these three norms.

As I develop these ideas some may wonder if such a task is ambitious enough, large enough to counter the precipitous social decline I have spent so much time describing. But that is the wrong question. In asking that question, we are attempting to articulate large-scale solutions that will fix the machinery of society. Thinking in these terms is precisely what got us into the mess we are currently in. Society is not a machine. Society is the sum total of human relationships and institutions. So we cannot find mechanistic solutions to the problems facing us. The problems are deeply human, and so too must be the solutions. Indeed, the prescription Christianity gives to individual people is no more complex, and yet we do not dismiss it as insufficient or impractical. We tell the drug addict, the corrupt politician, the gang member, and the thieving Wall Street banker the same thing: Repent, or you too will perish.

Why we would expect the faith's counsel to communities to be different is a mystery. We recognize here that the first step toward reunion with God is simply believing the promises of God as they are offered in the gospel and laying hold of Christ's righteousness by faith. This seems too easy to some, and yet it is where the Christian life begins. As the great Dutch theologian Herman Bavinck once said, "All good, enduring reformation begins with ourselves and takes its starting point in one's own heart and life."[2]

As we return to these practices, we will find that they answer the despair of modern humans. They give to us both a set of practices and the underlying principles that offer a coherent picture of life together. They help us to fashion a world in which love can be at home.

SIX

SABBATH AND THE
CHIEF END OF MAN

Turning and turning in the widening gyre
The falcon cannot hear the falconer;
Things fall apart; the centre cannot hold.

W. B. YEATS, "THE SECOND COMING"

FOR MUCH OF HIS CHILDHOOD in Vienna, Frederic Morton could not escape what he called "the factory." The factory, for Morton, symbolized the world of tedium, of work, of constantly striving under a heavy burden to prove oneself to one's parents. The noise of the factory was an ever-present companion to him. It "hums away, unstanched, inviolable. It hums in great metal halls, in shopping centers, on brownstone stoops, under post-graduate pipe smoke, on highways and around the coffee table."[1] The pressures it imposed were almost never far from his mind.

But that word *almost* is worth lingering over. Sometimes the factory was shut down. The noise stopped. The fear of his father's arched "weekday" eyebrows faded. Morton describes how it happened. He would come on Saturday afternoons to the actual factory where his father worked. He had a satchel with his school things in it, his "contribution" to the family's work. He would bring it to his father's rolltop desk, anxious over what his father would make of the work when he reviewed it. But then something would happen:

> He closed the rolltop desk over those inexorable papers and even over
> my satchel, the satchel which—though I no longer touched it—stung

my nerves. Yes, my father actually rolled down the rolltop with a definitive thunder, followed by the hissing creak of his key turning the lock. Those motions, those sounds were the beginnings of our approach toward the Sabbath.[2]

Morton and his father then went through the factory, locking up the doors, turning off the lights. His father often let Morton participate in this ritual, turning some of the locks himself as his father looked on. Then they went out into the Viennese streets. The work was over. The factory was silent. The sabbath had arrived.

THE FACTORY AND THE SABBATH

Hopefully it is not presumptuous to think that if you are reading this book, you are familiar with "the factory." If you have read to this point, you have at least seen it described in the previous pages. The factory is where our place is not assumed but must be earned through our effort. There is no meaning here, only striving and proving. We do not enjoy a given identity or sure place in its membership. It all must be obtained through effort. Flights of imaginative fancy and wonder at the world do us no good in its cold, metallic halls. The place is solid all the way through. And if the day comes when we are no longer needed, the owners of the factory will have no hesitation in casting us out onto the streets, cold and alone. We know the factory. And for Morton the first and best response to the gray impersonal factory is the sabbath. It's how we "lock out" the factory, if only for a while.

But do we today know the sabbath? Later Morton describes how his father would "smuggle" the sabbath into the factory. That, as a friend of mine said to me once, is the rightful work of God's people—to smuggle rest and hope and joy into places that know nothing of those things. But before we can talk about smuggling the sabbath into the factory, we must first have a clear idea of what the sabbath is. There are three aspects we must understand of the sabbath. First, we must see how the sabbath orients us toward the world of time. Second, we must learn to set aside the sabbath for public worship of God. Third, we must learn to see in the sabbath a glorious indifference to the factory, which is the inevitable consequence of orienting ourselves to time and, ultimately, to God.

THE SABBATH AND TIME

Writing in the prologue to his book *The Sabbath*, Rabbi Abraham Heschel says,

> To gain control of the world of space is certainly one of our tasks. The danger begins when in gaining power in the realm of space we forfeit all aspirations in the realm of time. There is a realm of time where the goal is not to have but to be, not to own but to give, not to control but to share, not to subdue but to be in accord. Life goes wrong when the control of space, the acquisition of things of space, becomes our sole concern.[3]

The sabbath turns our attention away from the world of space and the work we do within that and toward the work of time. This is something that many of us find deeply uncomfortable—and for good reason! In a world as captive to existentialism as ours, it is uncomfortable to reckon with the realm of time because time is the most obvious natural limitation that all our modern technological tools have not yet been able to overcome.

One way of reading modern history is as the story of how people have sought to free themselves from unchosen restraints. Cars free us from the constraints of geography, as do airplanes to an even greater degree. Air conditioning and electrical lights free us from the constraints of seasonality and evening and morning. The grocery store frees us from the constraints of agriculture and the need to work long hours simply in order to eat. And for much of our lives, this is sufficient. Because of these developments, there are long periods of our lives in which existentialism suits us. It makes no demands on us and offers us the occasional moment of transcendence, whether expected (as at a wedding or the birth of one's child) or unexpected (the first time we meet our future partner or, less seriously, the day our sports team wins a title or we hear a beloved band perform live). This is enough for most of us for much of our lives, particularly when our world affords so many material comforts and offers many at a low price. Netflix is $13 a month and can fill even the loneliest night in a not unpleasant way.

Yet for all our innovations, all our cleverness, all our techniques for expanding our freedom, there is one restraint we have been unable to transcend—time. Moreover, in pursuing personal, individualistic freedom to such extreme degrees, many of us have done great violence to our own souls and the souls of those around us. We have grown distant from friends and family. We have made immoral choices in the pursuit of professional success—fudging a detail on a résumé here, misleading a potential customer as we chase a sale over there. The pressures created by such a life build on us as we age. And so we approach time with fear, for we know somewhere in our bones that time will eventually reveal the ugliness we wish to hide, much as a painting concealed the ugliness of Dorian Gray's sin in Oscar Wilde's novel *The Picture of Dorian Gray*, in which a young man's wish that a painted portrait would age and he never would is granted. Time exposes what we have made of our lives, what we have done with our freedom. It exposes how far we have wandered from God. And so we would rather ignore it, we would choose instead to give ourselves to the world of space. The sabbath reminds us that we cannot carry on in this way forever.

That said, if we allow it to, the sabbath will do more than merely disrupt. In confronting our mortality, we quite reasonably confront the question of what it is to live a good life. And the sabbath directs our attention to the thing that would answer that question if we would submit to it: The end toward which we are made is to know God. We are made so we would become holy, as our Maker is holy, and then, in our holiness, serve others who share that vocation with us and offer to them a faint imitation of the love we receive from Christ. *That* is why we are made. That is the vocation—calling—given to all people. It is to look at our neighbor, imagine what they would be in a perfectly holy, happy state, and then to labor, with the help of the Holy Spirit, to guide them toward that end. Oscar Romero made this point provocatively, saying, "The vocation of human beings is to collaborate in the salvation of others."[4]

So as we confront the fact of time and our place in it, the sabbath also directs our eyes forward toward our rightful end as human beings, to God himself. Indeed, the mere fact of the sabbath rest should draw our attention toward God. We rest, after all, because God himself is described as doing it in Genesis and because we are made in his image and we too must rest. And that word *rest* makes all the difference in the world. When we observe sabbath, we are orienting ourselves to God, who we meet by faith.

The sabbath itself traditionally is a clear and costly picture of faith. When it was practiced by Jews during the wilderness wanderings, they *had* to rely on God to provide for them materially because their daily work is what sustained their existence and there was little margin built into their lives that could allow for an easy day of rest with minimal material consequence. By choosing not to work, the Israelites were saying to God that they trusted him to provide, that they would follow his command to rest even when doing so could mean they would not have food. And God did provide—on the day before the Sabbath he gave Israel a double portion of the manna, and the manna kept for two days rather than the normal one.

Once Israel occupied the land, the demands of Sabbath became more acute. In Leviticus 25, God calls on Israel to observe a Sabbath year once they enter the land. The practice required that Israel not sow any new seed during that year or prune any of the vines or other crops. To eat, they would rely on what grew wild on the land (food they had not planted but grew on its own) as well as food that had been harvested the year prior to the Sabbath year. Indeed, God promises them to make the harvest of the sixth year so bountiful that they can live off it during the sixth year, the Sabbath year, and then in the first part of the eighth year during planting season. Sabbath, then, is a practical lesson in trusting God to provide and resisting the temptation to take matters in our own hands. It is a master class in understanding the meaning of the famous biblical command to "be still and know that I am God" and to trust God in the ways that Christ describes in the Sermon on the Mount.

An emerging concern among evangelicals more generally is how we practice our faith in the practical matters of day-to-day life. This question is central to the work of James K. A. Smith and has occupied a number of lesser-known evangelical authors as well. So imagine the mental strain of practicing a sabbath year—to say nothing of a year of Jubilee!—and how that would test our faith. Every time we walk past the fallow fields is a reminder of the demands of the sabbath year. When we draw on the remains from the sixth year, we are reminded of God's care. And as we eat food grown in the wilderness we are reminded of the sacrifice involved in observing the sabbath. We are, ultimately, reminded of why we were made, of what our greatest good is. And we are drawn into the story that will equip us to call others toward the same good.

THE SABBATH AND PUBLIC WORSHIP

Yet there is more that should be said. After all, the world, and specifically the economy of Leviticus 25, is a long way from the twenty-first-century West. So what does sabbath mean for us today?

The answer is quite simple. Just as it always has, it means that this is a day when we order our lives toward God in a unique way that is distinct from the way we orient ourselves to him the rest of the week. And how do we do that?

Don't overthink it.

We go to church.

The most basic way we can observe and practice sabbath today is by participating in the public worship of God's people, united around the preaching of the gospel and participation in the sacraments. By placing public worship near the center of our sabbath practice, we are escaping the inevitably individualistic way many of us naturally think about spiritual disciplines, sitting down by myself in a chair with my Bible and beginning to read. To be sure, private Bible reading is a vital part of Christian piety. But for many American evangelicals in particular it has been emphasized in ways that tacitly devalue the gathered together public worship of God's people, united around Word and Table.

In public worship, we are by definition united with other people; I do not stand in the pulpit and preach. My pastor does. I do not dispense the sacraments; the elders do. I do not sit alone in a room and ponder the Scriptures; I sit together with other followers of Jesus and hear the Word preached. I do not pray the Lord's Prayer by myself but with the gathered people of God. I do not sing by myself; I sing with the aid of musicians and alongside parishioners who worship the same God I do.

This practice of public worship is an inherently social thing that breaks me out of my natural individualism. Indeed, it doesn't simply break me out of my individualism; it also forces me into contact with people I might not otherwise like very much if not for Christ. I will say the Creed with the woman who works for the politician I don't like and the man who once offended me with a rude remark. I'll share the Supper with a peer who does not share my theological views. And in taking membership vows I will submit myself to the loving discipline of a session or board that does not share all of my particular beliefs about how to organize daily life, approach Scripture, structure family life, and so on, *and* I will bind myself to a group of people who differ from me on all of those things as well.

In all these ways, public worship reminds me that I am not the master of my fate, that I am not the captain of my soul, that ultimately I am not my own, that I was bought with a price. Indeed, I am bound together in eternal communion with people I do not even particularly like right now, let alone love. But the gospel tells me that God loves them just as he does me. And so there is a reminder in the sabbath to forgive, to see that the perceived sin of my neighbor in the pew is no more beyond the reach of divine grace than my own sins.

This point is brought home in a particularly powerful way with the architecture of many old cathedrals. Many old European cathedrals, built during the high medieval era, were laid out in the shape of a cross with the entrance coming at what would, from the sky, look like the base of the cross. So people enter the church building at the foot of the cross. Moreover, many of these churches featured carved reliefs above the door showing Christ on the judgment seat. And so everyone who wishes to enter the church must do so at the foot of the cross and pass under the judgment of God. The physical space itself reminds us of who we are, who our neighbors are, and what we all need together.

The image of public worship also helps us to understand what the common good actually is. The common good has been much discussed in recent years, often within an explicitly political context and often in order to justify some political policy or another. But we seldom take the time to actually define what the common good is or to explain what it looks like in simple, nonpartisan terms.

The young Catholic writer Jose Mena explains the problem well. Mena says that many of us think of the common good like a pizza—it's this one big thing called "the good" that we all share among ourselves.[5] So I take a slice of it and go off and enjoy it, and you take a slice and enjoy it, and so on. And as long as the pie is sufficiently large, the common good is being served because everyone has a slice. But this is not at all how the common good has been traditionally understood either in antiquity or in the Christian tradition. The idea of a common good is that it is a good that *only* can be enjoyed in common with others. This is why the pizza illustration fails. When we think about a pizza, we can slice the pizza into individual slices that can then be taken and enjoyed fully by individual people. My experience of the pizza is not going to change based on whether I have the whole pie or a single slice. It's the same thing either way.

Common goods, in contrast, cannot be sliced up and served individually. They must by their very nature be held together with others. Thus they are less like a pizza and more like a symphony: If you remove the brass section from an orchestral piece, the piece is not the same. You need the entire symphony for the good of that musical composition to be fully enjoyed. It is not possible for the trumpet player to go off by himself, play only his part, and still experience the same good that he would were he playing in the orchestra.

Public worship works this way. If I go off by myself and attempt to replicate all of the service, it will not be the same. The sermon will be weaker, the sacrament robbed of much of its symbolic power, and the music will be a shadow of itself. In public worship we experience a common good—God's people bound together and fulfilling their calling as human beings collectively—and this is a rare and beautiful thing in a world in which community has been torn apart in so many ways.

Once we see public worship in this way, we are ready to push this point about the observance of the sabbath a bit further. When we say that on the sabbath we order our lives toward God in a unique way and that the easiest way of ordering them in this way is through public worship, we do not simply mean Sunday morning worship. For many Christians, our sabbath observation begins and ends on Sunday morning and the rest of the day looks like Saturday, basically—there are youth sports, professional sports events, perhaps some shopping, and maybe a bit of work around the house that didn't get done earlier in the week.

Without wishing to speak beyond what Scripture itself says, this seems to me both profoundly sad and deeply illustrative of our current crisis within the church. Many of us, myself sometimes included, find ways of fitting our religious practice into a schedule that is otherwise defined and controlled by other concerns and obligations. Yet this is not how it has always been. Traditionally, American evangelicals spent a far greater proportion of our Sundays in religious observance of some kind. Many churches had morning and evening services, a practice that has been almost entirely abandoned today. Indeed, the few churches that *do* offer evening services usually simply do the same service they did in the morning and offer the evening time as a way of dealing with overcrowding on Sunday morning or as a more convenient option for some of their congregation.

Thus, one way we might recover the sabbath today is simply by going back to two worship services on every Lord's Day. Having the sabbath bookended by public worship helps to underscore the centrality of worship to the practice of rest, as understood in Christianity. But it also helps us with something else, a problem less poetic and more mechanical.

The typical Sunday morning sermon is around thirty minutes. Assuming the preacher speaks at a normal rate of 100 to 150 words per minute, that's going to be between three and five thousand words. And that will be the sum total in spiritual instruction that many evangelicals receive in an entire week. Is it any wonder, then, that so many evangelicals are so theologically illiterate? Combine that with the lamentable numbers we have on how many books the average American (doesn't) read and you should have no difficulty understanding the low level of lay education in most American churches. This lack of biblical and theological formation is, of course, one aspect of the problems we discussed in chapter one: you are more susceptible to the many hucksters of American religious life if you do not understand true religion for yourself.

Sunday evening services offer a chance to provide further training in the faith for all Christians. Traditionally, the evening service was when a preacher might do a survey series through a more obscure part of the Bible, allowing the congregation to become acquainted with neglected parts of the Old Testament or a lesser known New Testament letter. In other cases, preachers might use the evening service to preach through a catechism. The Heidelberg Catechism, for example, is split up into fifty-two sections, so the pastor could work through the entire thing in a single year.

Some churches are beginning to recognize their error here. One friend told me that many churches in his area are beginning to return to evening worship services for precisely these reasons. "They realized that Sunday morning alone just wasn't enough time to train their people in the faith," he said. Indeed, Sunday morning worship is often not really *designed* to offer that sort of rigorous formation. If a preacher spends ninety minutes preaching through a short biblical text and wades too far into the weeds, his sermon has likely stopped being sensible to any visitors who showed up, curious to learn more about Christianity. Morning sermons probably shouldn't be more than thirty minutes and probably *should* stick to relatively straightforward presentations of the gospel as expounded through the text being preached on that day. Evening services provide the opportunity to preach more technical sermons and to create another context in which the congregation can come together for worship and hearing the truths of the gospel.

There is a final point in favor of evening services as well. A friend told me once about his alcoholic father's unlikely conversion following his encounter with Christ. Ever after, my friend said his family was in church twice on Sundays and once on Wednesdays, and they'd have been more often if they could. But this wasn't performative piety or an attempt to ingratiate themselves to the church. It was more basic. "My dad knew he needed it," my friend said. His father knew that the thing keeping him from a relapse was the grace of God. And so every chance he had to hear about that grace was a chance he wished to take. The public communing of God's people was not an item on a checklist for him, not a motion that he went through during his week alongside mowing the lawn, going to work, and visiting the grocery store. It was, rather, something essential to his well-being, something he *needed*.

THE SABBATH AND THE LITURGIES OF THE FACTORY

So far what I have said about the sabbath might seem narrow, particularly given that my argument is that the sabbath is a broader reminder about why we and our neighbors were made, a reminder of our status as human beings made in the image of God, possessing dignity and worth, and made to know and enjoy God forever.

Though "go to church" is better advice than many younger evangelicals might think, there is still the simple problem that even if we do give more of our sabbaths to public worship, that still leaves a great deal of time (even on the sabbath) that will not be spent in public worship. We will eat lunches, have some chunk of time free during the day, and then will return home to conclude the sabbath at the end of our day. What does it mean to honor the sabbath within that broader context of the entire day? And how does honoring the sabbath in this way answer the aimlessness and angst described earlier?

Here the example of L'Abri, a residential study center with a number of branches located around the world, can be instructive. The community at L'Abri follows a fairly strict rule for daily life. Five days a week are given to regular rhythms of work and study. During my time there as a student, work often was focused on the property—typically weeding—and hospitality work, cleaning, preparing food for meals, setting up for lecture and film nights, and so on. The other half of my day was set aside for study, principally reading but also meeting with a full-time resident at the community to discuss my reading and my time at L'Abri more broadly. Sunday is one of two days off during the week for students. The permanent residents attend church on Sunday morning with students having the option to stay or go to services.

A long, leisurely Sunday lunch follows the morning services. Sometimes we would listen to a symphony or listen to a story read aloud during our meal. (I was first introduced to the works of Kate DiCamillo and P. G. Wodehouse during my stays at L'Abri.) Then that evening we would have a high tea. High tea, a L'Abri tradition, is meant to be a way to conclude the sabbath with a time of beauty, reflection, and conversation. Because of the large lunch, no one was particularly hungry by supper time, so we would set out finger foods with small plates, and make several pots of tea. Then we would invite everyone from the church and surrounding community to join us. Some nights would include an open mic in which students were free to share poetry, play music, or read a story. On other nights a resident might read to us from a beloved book. And sometimes we just gathered without any particular plan and spent the evening in conversation.

Certainly, formal worship was a significant part of the sabbath at L'Abri, but the entire sabbath felt bathed in a glorious indifference to the affairs of the factory. It was not a day for performing or anxiety, for earning our status, for worrying over the possibility of failure. It was a day for dancing and singing and tea and talking. It often felt like something out of the Shire or perhaps the holidays at Hogwarts.

The point of the sabbath is not simply to set aside the day for formal worship, although we should. It is also to mark the day as a time for shutting out the factory and the idolatries it tempts us to. We hallow the Lord's Day through the offering up of the whole day to God, not just in formal worship but in the creative use of our home places to bless others with the rest that the creation account describes in Genesis 1. And when we do this, we begin to be shaped as the sorts of people who can enter back into the factory on Monday, smuggling in a bit of the sabbath with us.

SEVEN

THE MEMBERSHIP

IN HIS BOOK *SEARCHING FOR GOD KNOWS WHAT*, Donald Miller describes what he calls lifeboat communities. It's a thought experiment that raises a simple question: In communities that have a zero-sum understanding of common life, eventually you run into a limit and, well, someone in the community has to go. If there is only so much room on the boat and we can't take everyone, who is more valuable? Miller specifically shares a story from his school days when his class debated this question: "If there were a lifeboat adrift at sea, and in the lifeboat were a male lawyer, a female doctor, a crippled child, a stay-at-home mom, and a garbageman, and one person had to be thrown overboard to save the others, which person would we choose?"

Miller then describes how the debate went in the class.

> I don't remember which person we threw out of the boat. I think it came down to the lawyer, but I can't remember exactly. I do remember, however, that the class did not hesitate in deciding who had value and who didn't. The idea that all people are equal never came up. As I was saying before, we knew this sort of thing intrinsically. Or at least we thought we did.[1]

For lifeboat communities, we assume that the world is basically bleak and hostile. The only way to sustain our own existences in such a world is to fight for them. Nature is, as the poem goes, "red in tooth and claw" and will destroy us if given half a chance.[2] So be vigilant, watchful, and don't expect much. The world is a dull and dangerous place. Pile into the lifeboat. Fight for your spot. The world is not a membership, a place of interlocking lives that thrive together. It is a Darwinian wilderness where only those deemed fit can survive.

DISPOSABLE COMMUNITY

Many of us are familiar with this sort of community. We have firsthand experience with communities that see their members as being disposable or interchangeable. It's the middle school classroom that bullies a kid who has a disability or who comes from a poor home. We see it most clearly in the business world. In recent years Silicon Valley types have made a point of saying that a business is "a team, not a family." In an interview for the *Harvard Business Review*, several of them write,

> Consider another metaphor—one that Reed Hastings, the CEO of Netflix, introduced in a famous presentation on his company's culture. Hastings stated, "We're a team, not a family." He went on to advise managers to ask themselves, "Which of my people, if they told me they were leaving for a similar job at a peer company, would I fight hard to keep at Netflix? The other people should get a generous severance now so we can open a slot to try to find a star for that role."[3]

In case there is any doubt at how this thinking works out in practice, an NPR interview with a former Netflix executive should make clear where this sort of "community" ends up. In it, the executive, Patty McCord, describes how she excoriated an employee who had the temerity to cry upon finding out that she was being fired:

> So I called her up. I'm like, what part of this is a surprise? . . . We've been talking about this as a strategy for years. We've talked about this. And she goes, "Yeah, but . . . I've worked really hard; this is really unfair." I [said], "You're crying? . . . Will you dry your tears and hold your head up and go be from Netflix? Why do you think you're the last one here? 'Cause you're the best. You're incredibly good at what you do. We just don't need you to do it anymore."[4]

Later in the same interview, McCord complained about the word *fired* and suggested that we say people "move on" instead. When asked how many people she helped "move on," she glibly replied, "oh, hundreds."

Yet even if we wish to argue that such a practice may sometimes be defensible in the business world—if you don't have the money to pay a person, then something has to give—this same mentality pervades our approach to communal life more generally. Because of the disordered way we think about individual freedom, all of our communities end up mimicking the underlying logic of the lifeboat: "You're with me right up until you stop being useful or I just don't want your company anymore." This same mentality shows up when we talk about marriage. Thus the ascent of no-fault divorce, the growing comfort among millennials with prenuptial agreements, and even more fringe ideas like abolishing marriage as a lifelong commitment and replacing it with "marriage leases," which are exactly what they sound like, legal contracts of a fixed length in which two people agree to share their lives as legally recognized partners.

We also can see it in disturbing news stories, such as a recent report from Iceland that found the country has nearly aborted Down syndrome out of existence. According to a report from CBS, nearly 100 percent of babies in Iceland who test positive for Down syndrome in the womb are killed. This number is horrific, but not anomalous:

> Other countries aren't lagging too far behind in Down syndrome termination rates. According to the most recent data available, the United States has an estimated termination rate for Down syndrome of 67 percent (1995–2011); in France it's 77 percent (2015); and Denmark, 98 percent (2015). The law in Iceland permits abortion after 16 weeks if the fetus has a deformity—and Down syndrome is included in this category.[5]

The inclusion of Denmark in that list is also striking, for it is not only the unborn that the supposedly idyllic Northern European nation, which routinely is listed near the top of polls measuring the happiest nations on earth, has attempted to totally exclude from its population. Their disregard for the humanity of certain classes of people also extends to immigrants. In 2018, in response to the migrant crisis in Europe, the Danes passed a number of new laws that regulate how communities in majority-immigrant neighborhoods must act. These neighborhoods are, in fact, called "ghettos," which less than one hundred years after World War II should perhaps give people more pause than it has so far.

The proposed reforms include laws that stipulate that, beginning at age one, "ghetto children" must spend at least twenty-five hours a week outside of the home for "re-education" in "Danish values." Another proposal (this one did not pass) was that "ghetto children" be required to be in their homes after 8 p.m. with ankle monitors. This was proposed as a way of insuring these children are not out after curfew.[6]

In perhaps the most disturbing picture of this lifeboat-style community life, a group of Syrian refugees who actually *were* on a lifeboat in the Mediterranean Sea radioed to the Italian coast guard in a moment of desperation: "Please hurry, we are going down," said a doctor on the boat as he was desperately trying to find help after the boat, which bore 260 human souls, began taking on water. "We are dying, please," he added at the end of his call.

The Italian coast guard told him to call Malta. You see, though they were only sixty-one miles from an Italian island and an Italian boat was sailing between ten and nineteen miles away awaiting instruction, the coast guard reasoned that since they were *technically* in Maltese waters they were Malta's problem, not Italy's. British newspaper *The Independent* describes what happened next:

> Five hours after [the doctor's] initial call to the Italian Coast Guard, the fishing boat capsized, sending over 260 people, including 60 children, into the Mediterranean Sea. There is yet to be an official investigation into the 11 October sinking, with reports stating at least 34 refugees were confirmed dead. Around 147 survivors were taken to Malta and a further 56 taken to Italy.[7]

Even here, we have not exhausted the depths of the problem. In the big picture, our Darwinian impulses do not just hurt human life; they hurt plant life. The same view of the world that views people as disposable also views animals, trees, and streams in the same way. And so just as we think nothing of a company "moving on" hundreds of workers, we similarly think nothing of tearing up forests and woodlands, polluting streams, and destroying the habitats of countless animals. The disenchanted world is hostile to all forms of life, not just humanity.

This is the challenge before us. Our forms of "community" life more typically look like the lifeboat than anything else. They rely on a baseline logic of fear and power. And when push comes to shove—when accommodating *everyone* on the lifeboat would require something of us—we're happier to just shove someone off the boat. Community is a disposable good, we think, something we can dispense with when things begin to get a little tight. So we shove people and other living things off the lifeboat. The person we get rid of will vary, a friend that embarrassed us by doing something they themselves admit was stupid, a redundant employee, a spouse we no longer love, a disabled child, an immigrant. But the cruelty of the act remains. In fact, we should find a new word to describe these kinds of groups. Calling them a "community" is a disservice to what is still a good word. But is there an alternative?

THE MEMBERSHIP

The lifeboat metaphor is one picture of what shape our life together might take. It is a picture of community fashioned chiefly out of human vanity and fear, one that has no natural existence but only exists because of the ways human sinfulness misshapes our desire to be known and turns it toward perverse ends. It is, most of all, a community that we must qualify for.

This brings us, then, to the second thing that we must recover if we are to repair common life in our republic. We must recover what Wendell Berry calls "the membership." By recovering membership, we also recover something else: wonder. When we recover the membership, we recover the idea that we do not exist in the world as lonely, alienated individuals but as embodied creatures made by the same God who made the rivers and the animals and the mountains and the ocean. We see in the membership a reminder that the world has an order to it, that we are part of that order, and that the order is far larger than we are. And so it tells us both to walk gently and to rejoice. So as we talk about the membership, we are not simply talking about human communities but about the natural order created by God in which human beings live and work, we are talking about a world made and loved by God, and we are talking about the gifts that world offers to us and the responsibilities it assigns to us.

MEMBERSHIP IN SCRIPTURE

Membership, like sabbath, is something we can see described in the opening chapters of Genesis. It is seen when God looks at Adam and says, "It is not good for man to be alone." Note that this is *before* sin enters the world (chap. 3). The need for companionship is not something that has resulted from the fall, as if we only need other people as a way to console ourselves as we attempt to live in a cursed world. That's not the biblical teaching, which is that we are *made* with a need to be in intimate relationship with other people. Even in a world without sin, God says that Adam needs a companion. So he creates Eve and gives her to Adam. Adam's response is, in the original Hebrew, almost a love poem—"at *last*," he says when he sees her. (Feel free to hear Etta James dragging out each of those syllables as you read it.)

The image here is of a couple deeply at home in the world together because their own life mirrors the life of the garden. It is not simply that we have two people who like each other and have a sexual relationship. We have two people who are at home with each other *and* in their place. The health of one is indistinguishable from the health of the other. The relationship between the people and the connection they have to the place should be seen as a single synthetic whole; the two things can't *really* be separated without doing great violence to both. The "us" is greater than "Adam" or "Eve" just as the garden is greater than the individual trees and animals that fill it, and the *membership*, by which I mean the cumulative life of people and place together, is greater than them all.

But the community we're seeing in Genesis should not merely be thought of as the community of marriage, though marriage is obviously a large part of it. If their life together had continued in an unfallen state, more lives would have been added, children and the children of their children. Thus we would have had not only the love seen in marriage but the love seen in friendship too, all existing within the garden. The community is an organic whole in which the love between the members and for their place comes together like a symphony, like a common good.

Lifeboat communities assume that our most natural state is to be alone and autonomous. Relationship, then, is an unnatural thing, something we take up under stress and in order to help ourselves. The lifeboat mentality looks at a person, or a thing, and wonders only if that thing will benefit them. Will this person or thing make me richer? Prettier? Stronger? Happier? Then I must have it. If it will not, well, better to let it go.

The membership, in contrast, assumes that human beings are communal and gregarious by nature. We cannot live the good life alone. And so we do not evaluate relationships with an eye only toward what they offer us. Rather, the membership directs us to look at another life and ask, "What does it demand of me?" This can seem a small difference, but it filters out into everything. In lifeboat communities, an implicit individualism runs through the whole thing—the "community," such as it is, can be dropped quickly when trouble presses in. This says something important about the artificial nature of these communities. They are not called into being by the existence of a natural good, like family or the love between friends or a shared love of a common place. They are, rather, called into being because one person or group found that they needed the other enough to justify forming an official relationship with them. But these relationships are easily broken, friendships severed by jobs, careers disrupted by layoffs or outsourcing, marriages ended because one of the partners has found someone "better." These communities are brittle because their only ultimate reference point is the temporal happiness of the individuals on the lifeboat.

In contrast, the membership's referent is the other and the place in which the membership exists. Berry describes this beautifully in his novel *Jayber Crow*, in which he describes how a farmer named Athey Keith saw his relationship to his land.

> Over a long time, the coming and passing of several generations, the old farm had settled into its patterns and cycles of work—its annual plowing moving from field to field; its animals arriving by birth or purchase, feeding and growing, thriving and departing. Its patterns and cycles were virtually the farm's own understanding of what it was doing, of what it could do without diminishment. This order was not unintelligent or rigid.

It tightened and slackened, shifted and changed in response to the markets and the weather. The Depression had changed it somewhat, and so had the war. But through all changes so far, the farm had endured. Its cycles of cropping and grazing, thought and work, were articulations of its wish to cohere and to last. The farm, so to speak, desired all of its lives to flourish. Athey was not exactly, or not only, what is called a "landowner." He was the farm's farmer, but also its creature and belonging. He lived its life, and it lived his; he knew that, of the two lives, his was meant to be the smaller and the shorter.[8]

Though a well-maintained farm offers a particularly powerful image of this sort of community, we can take a similar idea and apply it elsewhere. Take my grandpa, who I mentioned in chapter one. He went to work with broken ribs because when he considered his life and his family's life, "he knew that, of the two lives, his was meant to be the smaller and the shorter." We might say the same thing of a city. My friend Susannah is a lifelong New Yorker who adores the city. There is no better way to make one's first visit into Manhattan than to do so escorted by someone like her. She calls your attention to the unique features of old skyscrapers, stone features carved by immigrants who possessed skills that have been lost to time. She tells you who has the best coffee and where the best bookstores are. She knows that of the two lives, hers and New York City's, hers will be the smaller and the shorter. But this does not degrade the individual; in fact it exalts him or her. It links that person's beauty to the beauty of the entire membership. Again, to borrow from Lewis, "the inside is larger than the outside."

The lifeboat theory of common life, which makes room for individual expression right up until it suddenly *doesn't*, degrades the individual both by isolating them from the world—the whole image of a lifeboat presupposes there *isn't* a world outside that boat—and by judging their entire value to the community on the basis of their usefulness. When their usefulness ends, so too does their time in the group. The membership view does not work this way. It says that creation is a coherent, singular thing and that all the individual lives that exist in it—plant, animal, and human—have a belonging to it that they share, a belonging which gives to them a vocation and an identity.

But the thing only coheres if we recognize that, between ourselves and the enchanted world we call home, our life is meant to be the smaller and the shorter. The great Dominican writer A. G. Sertillanges captures this truth memorably, "The universe fills man with its glory, and you do not know it. The star of evening set against the darkening sky is lonely, it wants a place in your thought, and you refuse to admit it. You write, you compute, you string propositions together, you elaborate your theses, and you do not *look*."⁹

Christianity would have us look at the lonely star in the darkening sky. It would have us worship God and be filled with the glory of his world. It tells us that this world has a natural structure to it, an order that, when accepted, will appear to us as the doorway to happiness and all good adventure. We need the membership because we need a place, and we need a community that presupposes that something deeper than mere human liking binds us all together. Christianity tells us that this is true and that all good human communities are merely a subset of the great community, what Berry calls "the great coherence," to which all humanity belongs by virtue of being creatures made in God's image and born into his world. This is what Scripture has in mind when, for instance, the psalmist says to us:

> The heavens declare the glory of God;
>> the skies proclaim the work of his hands.
> Day after day they pour forth speech;
>> night after night they reveal knowledge.
> They have no speech, they use no words;
>> no sound is heard from them.
> Yet their voice goes out into all the earth,
>> their words to the ends of the world. (Psalm 19:1-4)

Scripture regularly assumes that nature can speak to us in these ways. It is striking to consider how God answers Job at the end of the Old Testament book of Job. Repeatedly, God calls Job's attention to the natural world: "Look at the stars, look at the sea, look at the sunrise, look at these remarkable beasts I have made." God is "answering" Job's questions about evil and suffering not via a direct philosophical argument but via the testimony of nature. He is saying to Job, "There is something you can learn about me and about yourself simply by taking the time to look at the world and think carefully about it." Similarly, in the Sermon on the Mount Jesus repeatedly assumes that his listeners can look at birds and flowers and learn something true about the God who made them and about themselves. They remind us that we live in a coherent membership made by God and deemed by him to be good. Our true happiness consists almost entirely in our ability to delight in our creatureliness and to view the membership with affection and to treat it with care.

Theologian Norman Wirzba explains it this way: "Jesus is not a gnostic teacher who visits earth to impart a few special, body-despising teachings to a select few. Rather, he is the eternally existent One who from the beginning has been at work ordering creation from the inside, making it an intelligible whole capable of membership and life."[10]

Even though we now live after the fall, after the entry of sin into the world, we still have that same need. If anything, the need is made more acute by the arrival of sin. We have always needed the membership, in other words, but we especially need it in a world marked by sin. We need the membership so we know not only that our life matters but that we have a place in this world, even at our worst. We need to know that we are cared for, even in a world that seems solid and indifferent all the way through. And if we do experience that sort of love, we will likely soon realize that the world is not so cold and boring as we sometimes think. But coming to see that this is true can be a trial.

THE MEMBERSHIP IN CREATION

In his poem "Two Hangovers," the deep image poet James Wright lands on a picture that should help us answer that question. He describes looking out his window and seeing a small blue jay hopping up and down on a nearby branch. Wright notes that the bird can be so taken with delight in that moment for a simple reason: "He knows the branch will not break."[11]

When we give ourselves entirely to contentment and gratitude to God, we are participating in the life of his membership. This gratitude manifests itself in delight—picture the apparent joy of a single bird as it hops up and down on a branch. But how can we, who live in a sin-cursed world and know well the pain it can cause us, experience that delight springing from gratitude?

There is a relationship between delight and knowledge. *Because* he knows that the branch will not break, the blue jay can delight in the day, in the tree, and so on. So what knowledge would we need to have in order to abandon ourselves in the same way? John Calvin answers the question in the famous opening line of his *Institutes of the Christian Religion*. Calvin argues that the sum of all true wisdom is to have true knowledge of God and of ourselves. Yet, he continues, it is very difficult to distinguish between the two because humanity depends on God so intimately and so comprehensively that it is virtually impossible to speak of ourselves without speaking of God. Because "our very being is nothing else than subsistence in God alone," we cannot draw neat dividing lines between what we know about God and what we know about ourselves. Moreover, Calvin continues, every good thing that we receive in creation is meant to direct our vision toward God. Calvin writes that though those blessings which "shed like dew from heaven upon us, we are led as by rivulets to the spring itself."[12]

So what is the knowledge that frees us to abandon ourselves to entire delight, like Wright's brilliant blue jay? It begins with knowledge of God, but not, if we follow Calvin, an abstracted knowledge that exists chiefly in the form of sentences written out on dusty blackboards. Rather, it is through a knowledge of God revealed to us in part by these unceasing blessings he pours out on us daily. These things tell us something about God. Of course, if we are speaking of how we can attend to the physical world and learn something about God, we must attend to the incarnate Jesus Christ, the humble Savior who made himself nothing so his beloved could live, even going to his torturous death with joy.

Yet the witness of God to us through generously giving us good things does not *end* with the incarnation, crucifixion, and resurrection of Christ, even if those acts are the center of his giving. We also see and know that the Lord is good because it rains, because crops grow, and because the sun warms our cheek as we wander outside on a clear spring day. That's not me being poetic, by the way. That's Paul. When he is explaining the Christian God to the pagan and mostly uneducated Greeks of Lystra, he quite explicitly appeals to rain as an argument for God (Acts 14:17). So we know God through a consideration of his work in the world, through studying his creation. Scripture routinely assumes that we can simply contemplate the world and arrive at true knowledge about it—thus Jesus' regular appeals to nature in the Sermon on the Mount. And in knowing him, we rejoice in him.

Indeed, to misunderstand the natural membership we are placed in will lead us almost inevitably to misunderstandings about God. "They hold a plainly false opinion who say that in regard to the truth of religion it does not matter what a man thinks about the Creation so long as he has the correct opinion concerning God. An error concerning the Creation ends as false thinking about God," said the great medieval theologian Thomas Aquinas.[13]

TWO CALLINGS TO MEMBERSHIP

Of course, the Lord has many ways of teaching us about this membership, many ways of drawing our eyes toward the beauty of his world and the goodness of his law. As with the sabbath, we should not overthink this. Everyone is called to know and love God and neighbor. Taking a step down a level, we can also say that everyone is called to one of two vocations as a way of testifying to both the goodness and unity of creation under the lordship of Christ.

One calling is to marriage. We should be clear on what I mean by that because it is a confused term in our world today. Marriage is not simply a legally recognized romantic relationship between two consenting adults. Nor, indeed, is it simply a legally recognized romantic relationship between a man and woman, as many late twentieth-century conservatives seemed to have thought. Marriage, traditionally understood, was as much for the children that would follow from the couple's relationship as it was for the couple themselves. It was meant to make it more likely that the children would grow up in a stable, secure situation and thus have a better shot at being provided for materially and being personally happy. It is, thus, a relationship deeply implicated in the membership, for it is the relationship in which the membership can most obviously be sustained.

Put more conventionally, marriage is a covenant relationship between a man and woman designed to provide a stable place for children to grow up and for the couple to mature in love for one another. So the relationship is not a contracted thing between two parties who pledge to make each other happy. It is, rather, a covenant in which the two parties offer themselves freely to the other in hopes that the relationship will not only make the other glorious, which is to say that it will make them look more like Christ, but also in hopes that the relationship would itself be fruitful in the most literal sense possible. It is a relationship oriented toward the flourishing of the world, seen in the bearing of children and making of households. In this sense, the covenant between man and woman mirrors—as Paul saw quite clearly—the covenant between God and his people. Just as Christ yielded up his body for the good of his beloved, so too are the two parties in marriage called to the same.

This point needs to be stressed because the modern Christian marriage too often is treated in a way that implicitly hollows it of much of its meaning. For example, in Mark Driscoll's book *Real Marriage*, marriage is treated as a kind of container in which our sexual expressions and desires, whatever they may be, are made licit. The sexual relationship is extracted out of creation, out of nature, and is simply made into a way of manufacturing pleasure for the couple. This is why Driscoll argued that sodomy—anal sex—can be an appropriate form of birth control. You have sexual needs. You don't want to get pregnant. So, sure, why not?

The Christian church has almost unanimously condemned such views historically, but our understanding of marriage and sexuality has drifted so far from that historic view that something like Driscoll's obscene proposal can end up being taken seriously by Christian publishers. Traditionally the church has said—almost with one voice for the first nineteen hundred years of church history—that sexual relationships that are intended to be indefinitely sterile are, in fact, a perversion of the true meaning of sex. Clement of Alexandria, one of the earliest fathers of the church, condemns it quite clearly, as do Augustine and John Chrysostom. Thomas Aquinas is clear on the matter as well, saying that contraception is "clearly contrary to man's good."[14] Calvin and Luther, likewise, are both clear in their condemnation of it, with Calvin going so far as to say that it "quenches the hope of [a] family."[15]

Why have so many Christians viewed marriage and sex in this way? Because marriage is an image of the goodness of God's creation, and as such it mirrors that goodness in its own life through the sacrificial love of spouses for one another and, necessarily, through the fruitfulness of their relationship. When we make marriage something other than this, we are removing it from the membership and implicitly placing it in the lifeboat where spouses regard one another less as partners in the membership and more as a means of achieving their own ends and goals.

In other words, when we sterilize the marriage relationship, we necessarily transform it into something new, removing it from the economy of love and resituating it in the economy of modernity. Wendell Berry makes the point well in his essay "Feminism, the Body, and the Machine," writing,

> Marriage, in what is evidently its most popular version, is now on the one hand an intimate "relationship" involving (ideally) two successful careerists in the same bed, and on the other hand a sort of private political system in which rights and interests must be constantly asserted and defended. Marriage, in other words, has now taken the form of divorce: a prolonged and impassioned negotiation as to how things shall be divided. During their understandably temporary association, the "married" couple will typically consume a large quantity of merchandise and a large portion of each other.[16]

But not all of us will be called to the vocation of marriage. There is another vocation many of us are called to: celibacy. In his book *Resurrection and Moral Order*, Oliver O'Donovan writes of this alternative witness beautifully:

[The New Testament church] conceived of marriage and singleness as alternative vocations, each a worthy form of life, the two together comprising the whole Christian witness to the nature of affectionate community. The one declared that God had vindicated the order of creation, the other pointed beyond to its eschatological transformation. But the coexistence of the two within the Christian church did not mean a loss of integrity to either.[17]

In celibacy, the individual person bears witness to the goodness of God, announcing to the world that God's love is sufficient. They do not need to marry to experience love or to know the good life. They give flesh, literally, to something that otherwise exists only in the future. The celibate Christian's life directs our attention to the life to come in which all of God's people will behold him as he is and be bound to him fully and without the veil of sin separating them from the one they are made for. In this sense, the witness of celibate gay Christians is a particularly powerful picture of the sufficiency of Christ, of the truth that we ultimately live by, as Jesus says in the Gospels, "every word that comes from the mouth of God" (Matthew 4:4). Yet we err if we think that the witness of celibacy is one reserved for gay Christians. The witness of celibacy is a vocation available to all Christian people. Singleness enables people to serve Christ in unique ways by making themselves available to the church and to others in ways they could not if married. This, of course, is part of Paul's argument for the good of celibacy in 1 Corinthians. The celibate Christian, freed from the concerns inherent in family life, can more easily offer themselves up to their fellow Christians and to those outside of the church.

Of course, there are obstacles to celibacy, particularly in our own culture. We have already discussed the challenge of loneliness. A celibate life is not the same as a life removed from all community. The celibate person is not rejecting *community* but simply one particular manifestation of human community. Often in our world, however, the only long-term local relationships that people have are their romantic relationships. So for gay Christians in particular, the calling to celibacy can come as a great burden. In one sense, this is inevitable for the simple reason that fulfilling God-given vocations in a sinful world is always a challenge. But there are things that Christian communities can and should do to help fight the battle against loneliness. Practices like families inviting celibate people to live with them are worth considering. Similarly, as much as possible it is a good idea for Christians to think carefully about where they will live before making a move. If it is possible, it is preferable to live within walking distance of Christian friends. This makes it easier to throw open your doors and offer hospitality to brothers and sisters in Christ. Similarly, churches should consider how they talk about singleness and also whether they are doing things that unintentionally make it harder for unmarried people to be included in the local Christian community. If women's ministries have most of their main events during the work day, for example, that will make it difficult for many unmarried women who have day jobs to attend—or married women with day jobs, for that matter. Likewise, if singleness is spoken of as a temporary state that one is constantly hoping to escape by finding a spouse, it can strengthen the gay Christian's sense of despair and also leave all the unmarried people in the church, gay or straight, feeling as if their life right now is happening in a kind of holding pattern, as if "real" life will not begin until they marry. This is not how it should be. The apostle Paul spoke highly of the celibate life, after all.

Many of the church's greatest leaders throughout her history— Augustine, Thomas Aquinas, and the Puritan theologian Richard Sibbes, author of the devotional classic *The Bruised Reed*—lived celibately for much or all of their life and ministry. So did C. S. Lewis, Mother Teresa, Amy Carmichael, Dorothy Day, and the great Anglican pastor and evangelist John Stott. We should not regard the vocation to celibacy as an incomplete or secondary calling.

In both of these callings, marriage and celibacy, we can see a life that is ordered toward the membership, toward an integral relationship between humanity, creation, and the God who made both.

CONCLUSION

When we think of community in terms of the modernist story—as a lifeboat we share with others until either they or we cease to be useful

—we ultimately devalue and destroy a great deal of God's world and the people he has made. This is a tragedy in itself, of course. Destroying something good and beautiful is a grievous thing. But it is also tragic because it cuts off those of us in the lifeboat from the people and places that might have directed our vision to Christ.

The comedian Jeremy McLellan once told a story of how God used a disabled man to get his attention just before a church service began.

> Yesterday I went to mass in Chicago and before the service in the restroom some guy with Down syndrome splashed me with water, soaking my shirt, let out the biggest laugh I'd ever heard, then ran out.
>
> I had so much on my mind, I had just prayed the rosary, I felt very spiritual and serious, then this dude just drags me back to reality and throws a giant wrench into my day. It was amazing.
>
> Later, during mass, the "peace" lasted about 10 minutes because everyone in his group of about 15 people with disabilities ran around greeting literally everyone in the church. It was normal to everyone. This is what they do. It was beautiful.
>
> I worked with people with disabilities for 15 years. One of the things I miss most was the beautiful anarchy. They humble you, drag you into reality. Hauerwas calls them "friends of time" because, to be friends with them, you must enter into their rhythms, their sense of time.
>
> We spend so much time thinking we don't have enough time, and so we violently cram others into our schedules and treat surprises (like getting soaked) as intrusions. Which they are! But living at peace with others requires welcoming such intrusions with hospitality.[18]

The Catholic writer Henri Nouwen—another celibate Christian—writes beautifully about this in his book *Adam*. The book is the story of Adam Arnett, a friend of Nouwen's who lived in the L'Arche community in Toronto. Due to a series of health complications as a child, Arnett was severely disabled and needed round-the-clock care. At L'Arche, Nouwen or another resident in the community would wake every day at 7 a.m. to help Adam with his morning routine—showering, shaving, dressing, eating breakfast, and so on. Then they would take him to the day program, where he would be until 4 p.m. with other L'Arche residents. The witness that the disabled offered to people like Nouwen was transformative, a fact brought home to Nouwen quite clearly in the story of Cathy, a wealthy, well-connected New York socialite.

Cathy came to L'Arche because she was depressed. She had accumulated an enormous amount of wealth as well as prestige over a long life in a major US city. And yet none of her success made her happy. "Gradually a most unusual but tragic picture emerged. Here was a woman who had everything a human being can dream of—money, fame, connections, and great power—wondering whether anyone really loved her. Rich but poor. Famous but self-doubting. Great but very small."[19]

As she spoke with the residents, one of them asked her, "Cathy, do you believe that you are a good person simply because you are Cathy?" She replied, "I don't know. I don't even know who I am without all the stuff that surrounds me. I don't know what it would mean if people loved me simply as Cathy. Would they? I often wonder!"[20]

Considering this story, Nouwen writes, "Cathy was asking the same question we all are asking: If people knew us as we really are, without all the worldly decorations we have gathered, would they still love us? Or would they forget us as soon as we were no longer of use to them?"

The life of the community at L'Arche offers an answer to that question. It reorients the people who visit to the simple truth that their dignity as a human is not contingent on their ability to prove their worth via displays of competence, wealth, or power. Rather, their membership is secured by their being created in God's image and belonging to the created order he loves. We see the membership when we slow down enough to see that God is at work in the world, not chiefly through the great and the powerful and the wealthy, but more often through the things that are hidden, the things that inconvenience us, the things that make demands of us. And yet the gospel tells us it is only in those places where we will find life, for "whoever tries to keep their life will lose it, but whoever loses their life will preserve it" (Luke 17:33).

EIGHT

WORK

To live, we must daily break the body and shed the blood of Creation. When we do this knowingly, lovingly, skillfully, reverently, it is a sacrament. When we do it ignorantly, greedily, clumsily, destructively, it is a desecration. In such desecration we condemn ourselves to spiritual and moral loneliness, and others to want.

WENDELL BERRY, *THE GIFT OF GOOD LAND*

ON A COOL JULY MORNING LAST YEAR I got up at 4:45, willing myself (very slowly) out of the comfortable bed and upstairs from the basement to the kitchen. I grabbed a lighter and went outside to the deck on the split-level house where my friends and I were staying. As I opened the door I practically walked into a wall of sound—the sounds of the world waking up. The home was on a hill overlooking the Pecatonica River in rural Illinois. The sounds merged together in such a way that I have no clue how many animals there were or even what specific kinds of birds I could hear. It felt like walking into a room full of small children on the last day of school eagerly talking about their plans for the summer. Even if you wanted to quiet them—which you should not—you wouldn't be able to. Besides the animals, I could see a fog hovering over the river and creeping up onto the banks in places. "And the Spirit of God hovered above the waters." John Stott, an avid bird-watcher, once spoke about the pleasures of being up at this time. "It is so marvelous to go out early in the morning before the world is awake," he said, "to enjoy all the sights and the sounds and the smells of nature, to be away from people."[1]

After taking a minute to just look and see what was there—city-dweller that I am, I was not used to the sounds that greeted me as I walked onto the porch—I found a small metal cylinder and filled it with charcoal. Then I set the cylinder inside a grill, crunched up a few pieces of paper and stuck them underneath the cylinder, and lit them. While the coals caught, I went inside and got a ten pound hunk of meat called a "pork butt." (It's actually meat from the shoulder of the pig.) I had already spent a bit of time with it the night before, trimming it, making my sauce, and sprinkling some salt on it. The salt, when applied that way, penetrates the meat and both adds flavor and retains moisture. I set it on a plate next to the grill. Then I got a large bowl full of a sauce I had made— vinegar, pepper, apple juice, brown sugar, ketchup, hot sauce, and a few other things. I gave it a stir and also set it next to the grill. Then I waited.

After the coals were ready, I dumped them out into the grill, pushed them all onto one side, and tossed a few chunks of wood into the bed of burning coals. Then I put the top grate on the grill. The pork went on the top grate on the side opposite from the coals. This is how to smoke meat using a basic charcoal grill—coals on one side, which create the heat, chunks of wood tossed into the coals, that makes smoke, and then the meat pushed to the other side of the grill, where it can cook at a lower temperature since all the heat reaching it is indirect radial heat coming from the coals on the other side of the grill.

Over the next twelve hours, I'd brush a bit more sauce onto the meat every hour. I added more coal about two-thirds of the way through the cook. And after twelve hours of cooking at that low temperature— roughly 250 degrees, though I didn't have a thermometer to check the grill's temperature so I can't know for sure—the pork was ready. I brought it inside, pulled it, and we were ready to eat.

TECHNIQUE VERSUS SACRAMENT

The funny thing about the method I just described is that, relatively speaking, it's the lazy person's method of barbecue. Pit master Rodney Scott of South Carolina (a pit master is just a chef who cooks barbecue) is more old-school, and *his* method shows how intensive the work can be. Scott's work begins by going out to the farms and acreages owned by his friends and neighbors to chop up trees they are donating to his restaurant. He takes a large truck and a chainsaw, and drives out to the place himself to cut up the wood and load it in the truck. Then he drives back to his restaurant, unloads all of it, and splits it. With that done, he tosses the wood into a burn barrel—which is just a burned-out old metal drum specially repurposed for Scott's work. The drum has a small door cut in the bottom, large enough for a shovel to fit through, and a number of circular holes cut throughout with old tire axles shoved through them. He then builds a fire in the top of the burn barrel. Once the wood has burned down to embers, the embers fall between the tire axles to the bottom of the barrel. From there, he scoops it out of the bottom with a shovel and takes it to the pit where the meat will cook.[2]

The "pit" is a long rectangular cinder-block structure with, again, a couple gaps left in the bottom of the side walls. On top of the pit a whole hog is laid out. Scott puts the coals underneath the legs and the shoulders and that's how the meat cooks. Eventually he'll turn the hog over so the skin is down and facing the coals. That's when he adds any spices or sauce he wants to put on it. Once the skin starts to pucker, he knows he's done. He brings the hog inside and his mother pulls all the meat, which they then serve their customers.

There's joy in this sort of work. I've never attempted anything quite as hardcore as Scott's approach, but even in the dabbling I do, I can find that joy. When our work is done skillfully and with regard for the creation, it takes on a new sort of quality. I see the wood burning and am reminded that someone somewhere chopped down the wood. Someone else built the grill or the pit I'm cooking on. Someone raised the pig. And now I, through patience and skill—if I have sufficient quantities of both and the right equipment—can take their work (and the pig's sacrifice) and turn it into something marvelous, something that will give delight to others. The physical objects become a conduit of something greater, which is of course what the sacraments are and is why Berry refers to this lesser work as "sacramental." I think he's right.

In contrast to this sort of work, we can consider what French philosopher Jacques Ellul called "technique." In his book *The Technological Society*, Ellul describes the ascent of technique with growing concern for what that rise will mean for people and society. The word *technique* has, of course, the same Greek root as the word *technology*, and if we begin by noting that commonality then we will be on our way toward understanding it. When we work according to technique, our concern is less to work skillfully and with understanding of the raw material set before us. Technical work presupposes the disenchanted universe of self-defined people, which I have already sketched out. Technique simply looks at those ideas and says, "Very good. If that is true, then the world is our sandbox. We can make whatever we want. We can use the earth however we want." Thus the goal is not symbiotic work geared toward the flourishing of neighbor and creation together. Rather, the goal is to use particular tasks and tools (our technology) to extract what I want from creation to secure my own peace and comfort. It's a sort of brute-force method that is indifferent to material, other people, or any innate hidden quality in the world. It is, rather, simply the means by which people assert themselves, express themselves, and gain mastery over the world.

In his book *The Year of Our Lord, 1943*, Alan Jacobs explains Ellul's understanding of technique by saying that "this outlook depends on two essential commitments: to efficiency, and to objectivity."[3] The basic belief is that the world and all that is in it is so much raw material—there is no inherent, essential qualities to it—and so we can use methods and technology to make of it whatever we like. Jacobs then notes that Ellul's work in this area was simply building off the work of earlier Christian critics such as the French philosopher Jacques Maritain, French mystic Simone Weil, and English poet W. H. Auden, among others. The fear these writers shared with Ellul is that the work of technique would, given time, deface creation and by necessity humanity. Oliver O'Donovan's description of technique is helpful.

> What marks this culture out most importantly is not anything that it does, but what it thinks. It is not "technological" because its instruments of making are extraordinarily sophisticated (though that is evidently the

case), but because it thinks of everything it does as a form of instrumental making. Politics (which should surely be the most non-instrumental of activities) is talked of as "making a better world"; love is "building a successful relationship." There is no place for simply *doing*.[4]

Recall Thomas Aquinas's words that errors in how we regard creation inevitably lead to errors elsewhere. Aquinas is specifically thinking about errors in how we think about God the Creator, but if we fail to rightly understand one realm of God's creation it is inevitable that we will misunderstand others, including ourselves.

WHAT IT MEANS TO WORK SACRAMENTALLY

This, then, is the challenge set before us. If the world is not a cold and indifferent mass of material but is instead the theater of God, and if human beings are not lonely and isolated but instead bear the divine image and the high calling to love God and neighbor, then how does that change the way we work? If we should *not* work according to the rules of technique, how *should* we work? There are three key ideas we need to have if we are to develop an attitude toward work that bears a closer resemblance to the Christian story and less of a resemblance to the modern story.

The goodness of work. The first point we must be clear on is that work is good. Work is something God gives to humanity before the fall described in Genesis 3. In a perfect world free from sin, it is simply normal and expected that people would work. Indeed, we might even say that work is one of the points of Adam and Eve's entire existence in the garden. They are placed in that garden not only to enjoy it but to tend, cultivate, and steward it. Because God loves Adam and Eve, the very things they are given to work with are the things that, given intelligence and skill, will make their lives comfortable and the place beautiful.

"Thus man was rich before he was born," writes Calvin.[5] It's a poetic thought but also a true one—by virtue of being born into the world we inherit at birth a certain kind of wealth. That wealth is the creation itself. We might even say that God expects Adam and Eve to *change* the garden and make it look different than it did when he was done with it after the sixth day of creation. This is because humans, being made in God's image, are creative. This is the work Adam and Eve were called to do: to be fruitful and multiply not only by having children but to be fruitful in how they worked the garden. The Garden of Eden was not intended to be a static place that stayed the same as it was when Adam and Eve first came to it, world without end.

Rather, it was given to them in a state that was without sin but also not finished. It was expected that Adam and Eve would work in the garden, improving it, making it more beautiful, and growing it. One of the first things we learn about God in Genesis is that he brings order to that which is chaotic and peoples that which had been empty. We find "the Spirit of God" hovering over the waters, and the creation days themselves are organized in three dyads, with the first half of the dyad referring to the creation of some kind of substance and the second half referring to the creation of the beings to fill it—so day one gives us light and dark, and day four gives us the sun, moon, and stars. Day two gives us the sea and sky, and day five gives us fish and birds. And then day three gives us the land, and day six gives us land animals and humans, the crown of creation.

This work to bring order to chaos and fill matter with persons was not only the work of God as described in the opening chapters of Genesis; it is also the work of men and women given to them by the God they are called to imitate. If we look to the end of Scripture, we see a number of the same agrarian images that confront us in Genesis 1–2. The tree of life, which first appears in the creation account, returns in Revelation. Yet it is worth noting how the Revelation language differs as well. We have moved from garden to city. That city is the fruit of humanity's work, done under the kind hand of God and empowered by his love. Thus we come to the point: work is itself good.

For many Americans, a different attitude about work prevails. It is a necessary evil, the thing you do to pay for your hobbies or, in more dire situations, to simply provide food and shelter. Thus work is a grinding pain we tolerate because it affords us the chance to enjoy many pleasures every weekend. To be sure, a large part of this aversion to work is not without reason. It is hard to feel enthusiasm for work in which a person has minimal freedom to make their own decisions about how to do a task and in which they are under constant surveillance, two qualities that describe a great deal of the jobs people now do in the United States.

That said, the overcorrection many of us make to the preponderance of alienated labor in the contemporary United States is to have a wholesale aversion to work, balancing out the hours of tedium with similarly empty hours spent at home browsing through Facebook on one's phone or zoning out in front of Netflix or Hulu. Contrary to this approach, which ironically devalues work and leisure alike, we must say that work itself is good and a normal part of creation, even prior to the arrival of sin in the world.

This work does not apply only to manual labor or work done in the marketplace. It also applies to things like the domestic arts of cooking, cleaning, and maintaining the economy of the home. This "work" is an opportunity we have to dignify a space, to delight human beings made in the divine image, and to create beauty that can refresh others. In her book *The Hidden Art of Homemaking*, Edith Schaeffer tells the story of how we can use the simple domestic arts of preparing food and setting a table as a way of showing another person our care and affection for them.

> There was a railroad running through the town. . . . Often hobos or tramps—rather derelict looking older men, unshaven and ragged of clothing, who travelled by riding on the bottom of freight cars or hidden inside an empty one—came to our back door, asking "Cup of coffee, ma'am, and maybe some bread?"
>
> "Wait a minute," I'd reply, "just sit down there, I'll fix you something." It was too dangerous to invite such a stranger in, alone with small children; but it would have been wrong to send him away. I would get out a tray, put the kettle on, and look in the fridge for some left-over soup. Into a small pan would go the soup, with the gas on under it. I would cut bread, enough for two big sandwiches (not too thin, he'll be hungry) and wonder what sort of a home he had had when he was a little boy—and wonder who he is, or whether maybe he is an angel in disguise! I would butter the bread, cut a lovely big tomato in even slices and pepper them, place them on the bread, and then decide to add bacon. I would sizzle one slice to fold over the tomato and add two leaves of lettuce. For a second sandwich

I'd prepare him my own favorite: walnut halves stuck into the butter, salted on one slice, and then the second piece of buttered bread placed on top. A diagonal cut through the first sandwich showed red tomato and green lettuce attractively displayed in the slash. The walnuts crunched as the knife went diagonally through the second sandwich. Alternating these four triangles on a lovely dinner plate came next, with pickle trim on one and parsley on the other. Now for the steaming hot soup left over from our lunch. I would put a good bowl of this on the tray, and the children would help me fix a tiny bouquet of flowers nested in an ivy leaf.

"What'll he think of all that, mummy?" Priscilla would ask with big, wondering eyes.

"Well, perhaps he'll remember something in his past—perhaps he had a very nice home once, where he had meals prepared for him. Anyway, he'll stop and *think*, and we'll give him this little Gospel of John to read while he is eating. He can take it away with him and, who knows, perhaps he'll do a *lot* of thinking, and some day, *believe*. Anyway, he may realize we care something about him as a person, and that's important."

Priscilla would hold the screen door open as I took it out, and watch his surprised face as he saw the tray.

"For *me*? Is this for me?"[6]

When we see our work as a good thing God gives us to do so we can bless our neighbor, it is inherently empowering; it gives us agency and encourages us to be creative in thinking of ways to dignify others. Many people would have simply ignored the homeless man at the door or pretended they weren't home. Most of us, myself included, I think, might answer but simply give the man whatever we had on hand that could be given without requiring any work from us—yeah, I have a can of Pepsi in the fridge and a granola bar. I can give him that. But Edith, understanding that the purpose of her work in their home was not simply to maintain a *space* but to make a *home* that would bless everyone, saw in that homeless man an opportunity to work for his good. And so she prepared a meal—note that none of it took much time or work. Making sandwiches, warming up some soup, and then taking two minutes to think about how to arrange them attractively—the sandwiches aren't simply thrown on a plate; they're sliced and arranged. And all of that told the homeless man that he was seen, that he was valued, that he was loved. Work done well is work that communicates love.

Sacramental work produces wealth. Second, sacramental work is ordered toward producing wealth. This will sound familiar, but there is a key caveat: wealth is not synonymous with money. The first and primary form of wealth is life. Good work is ordered toward life. It is responsive to the life of creation but also to the life of neighborhoods and homes.

To be sure, such work often will have a market value. Rodney Scott, after all, has made a living for himself selling his barbecue. But the ordering is important. Good work promotes life, which discerns the needs of people and place, and stewards a person's knowledge, abilities, and resources to promote the health of both. Harrison Higgins, a Virginia carpenter, describes the nature of such work in a remarkable video *Christianity Today* made in 2012 about his work. In it, Higgins distills the attitude of sacramental work down to its essence: "You save the best lumber for pieces that are worth that piece of lumber. You want the furniture to measure up to the lumber, to the tree that it came from. We want what we build from that tree to be worth what that tree was."[7]

The work of technique—with its emphasis on efficiency—will *generally* undermine our ability to do such work. And through its influence on the economy it will push more and more of us away from this kind of work. In the technique-driven economy, much of the actually creative work we do, work requiring unique skill and knowledge to be done well, is devalued in the name of efficiency. In a certain narrow economic way, this makes sense of course. We can produce more widgets if we use machines to speed up work or use methods that increase the rate people are able to work at. But this work comes at a spiritual cost to us.

Take the example I opened this chapter with. The pork required thirteen hours of my attention to cook properly. Every hour I had to sauce it, and for the last four to five hours I also checked the temperature with a small probe thermometer in multiple places on the meat. It also took time and money to acquire the ingredients and tools required to cook it, to say nothing of the knowledge needed to know how to do the various parts of the work. Viewed purely in terms of efficiency, this is all quite irresponsible. Viewed objectively, there are more financially remunerative ways I could use my time. But here we must respond like Charles Bingley does in *Pride and Prejudice* when his sister Caroline remarks that balls would be more rational if there was less dancing and more conversation. "Much more rational, I dare say," he says, "but it would not be near so much like a ball."

To criticize the work I was doing on grounds that it was inefficient is to miss the point: the goal was not to be *efficient* but to offer a gift to my friends. Whatever efficiencies that existed in the work—using store-bought wood for the smoker, for example—are done in service to a greater end than simply making money. When work becomes inordinately concerned with efficiency, much of this spiritual significance in work is lost because many of the things that make work feel meaningful to us require time, knowledge, patience, and a host of other qualities that often get on badly with efficiency. In a worst-case scenario that plays out far too often in the United States, work becomes focused purely on the earning of a wage or the generation of income, and it gradually becomes disconnected from life, which is the more primary form of wealth.

Writer Sarah Perry describes the problem well. Technology, she says, decondenses the physical world. "It abstracts a particular function away from an object, a person, or an institution, and allows it to grow separately from all the things it used to be connected to."[8] Put in more concrete terms, the meat I offered to my friends was more than simple nutrition. That meal represented my affection for them as proven by the time and expense put into preparing the food. It wasn't just a meal, in other words, but a physical signifier of my affection and love for my friends. This is what our grandmothers mean when they talk about love being the secret ingredient in their beloved family recipes. That food is not simply fuel or ballast, but something far more significant. It has a density to it, in other words—it signifies many things.

Decondensation is not necessarily bad in itself. After all, if the pulled pork I made my friends was denser, in this sense, than a Happy Meal, food grown by people in 1000 BC for their families was denser still—it symbolized time, knowledge, and care. The argument I am making is not that technical work is always and everywhere wrong in itself or that decondensation is always and everywhere wrong. It is not that simple.

Rather, the issue is that technical work's normal trajectory is to draw more and more of human life into its grip. Efficiency-obsessed capitalists are not good at recognizing where added efficiencies are useful and where they actually are alienating to worker, customer, or both. In contrast, a Christian theory of work is going to say that in certain ways it is good to make our work more efficient, but it will also mark out large swathes of life as off-limits to those concerns. Family dinners are both inefficient and good. Christian thinking along these lines helps us to hold these values together. But when we lack a belief in the goodness of work and the given created order, we lose the ability to balance the goods and cannot say when added efficiencies are worth pursuing and when they are not.

It would be one thing if we used technique in limited ways to help us work more effectively to better serve our neighbors. Sometimes it does, of course. But technique never stops at *that*. It pushes the boundaries of what is and is not subject to technique until even human identity itself is a thing to be shaped through it. I mean that quite literally, for what else is gender reassignment surgery, for example, but the use of a technique to construct a new identity from the raw material furnished by a person's body? Or, to highlight the problem on the other end of the political spectrum, what is something like strip-mining but the use of a technique to "free" people from the "confines" of their ordinary life by making cheap energy more readily available to them, even at the cost of literally dynamiting mountains and poisoning mountain streams?

Work that produces wealth, which is also work that promotes life, uses the flourishing of places and people as its primary point of reference rather than primarily looking at a bank account or some other financial number. There will be times—indeed, I rather suspect there will be *many* times—when work that promotes life will make uncomfortable and challenging demands on our pocketbooks. But this is the demand of our work, if we are to work in ways that elevate the creation and honor the God who made it.

Sacramental work is attentive to the membership. This final point will require a bit more work to unpack. To begin, we all know that God's benediction over work in Genesis 1–2 is not the last thing the Bible says about work. In Genesis 3 God pronounces a curse on the earth and the human body, which also afflicts our work. After the entry of sin into the world when Adam and Eve eat from the tree of knowledge of good and evil, God tells both of them that the work he has given them to do will now be toilsome and difficult. Our labor in the world will now be difficult and will require the literal breaking of the earth and of our bodies. This can still be done reverently and in ways that agree with God's design, but the difficulty is not a small point. Yet this is not the only way our work is touched by sin.

The human heart is also changed at the fall. A sin nature becomes attached to humanity like a parasite. It causes people to curve inward on themselves, as Luther said, or to become bent, to use Lewis's image. And we take this bentness into the way we work. This point brings us to the chief problem with much of the recent reflection on work by evangelical writers. One pastor, attempting to argue out of the broad framework of the Protestant doctrine of vocation, argues that "No matter what you do, your job has inherent purpose and meaning because you are doing it ultimately for the King. Who you work for is more important than what you do."[9] In this understanding, work is good, it is hard because of sin, but the difficulty is overcome through an intellectual exercise in remembering that you are working for Jesus and his glory.

This, unfortunately, is both a common way of thinking among some proponents of the faith-and-work movement *and* a drastic oversimplification of the biblical teaching on work. The issue is not just that work *itself* is toilsome after the fall but that the people doing the work are themselves curved inward, focused on their own desires and comfort rather than the divine call to love their neighbor. And so not only is good work toilsome but there is also such a thing as *bad* work.

Work that violates the moral law is obviously bad. There is no case to be made for the goodness of robbing banks for a living provided you convince yourself you're doing it for Jesus. Similarly, everyone recognizes that even good work can be done for the wrong reasons, which could end up causing it to become bad work.

But we should probe the idea of bad work more carefully. Certainly the moral law will define some forms of bad work, and motivation can explain how individuals can turn work bad through the orientation of their heart as they do the work. But neither of these criteria speak to the trajectory of work. Yet that question—to what end do you work?—may well be the most essential question of all because it encompasses questions about the basic morality of the work as well as the worker's motivation, but it also brings in far more.

Take telemarketing as an example: the telemarketer's job does not violate the moral law. And we can easily imagine a telemarketer who has good motivations for doing their job. They want to make money because they want to provide for their family. That is a good motivation! So is telemarketing a good job? To answer the question we should ask a different question: If a job ceased to exist, would anyone notice?

Anthropologist David Graeber discussed the phenomenon of such jobs, which he terms "bullshit jobs," in a widely discussed 2013 essay that led to the publication of a book with the same title. In the essay, Graeber argued that many of the jobs we have today are "bullshit jobs" because they are utterly unnecessary to the welfare of society.

> Say what you like about nurses, garbage collectors, or mechanics, it's obvious that were they to vanish in a puff of smoke, the results would be immediate and catastrophic. A world without teachers or dock-workers would soon be in trouble, and even one without science fiction writers or ska musicians would clearly be a lesser place. It's not entirely clear how humanity would suffer were all private equity CEOs, lobbyists, PR researchers, actuaries, telemarketers, bailiffs or legal consultants to similarly vanish. (Many suspect it might markedly improve.)[10]

Graeber's point is not to pass judgment on people who are convinced their work is meaningful. He is, rather, wrestling with a striking phenomenon: many of the people working in the positions he listed actually acknowledge the meaninglessness of their job. According to data from YouGov, 50 percent of British people either say their work makes no meaningful contribution to the world or that they aren't sure if their work makes a meaningful contribution to the world.[11]

The problem here is not with the moral nature of the work. Nor is it one of individual motivation. The problem is that the work is indifferent to the membership, indifferent to the order of interlocking life that God has made and called on humanity to steward, conserve, and nurture. This is not about heaping scorn on the people working these jobs—they themselves think their jobs are pointless!—but rather lamenting the fact that these jobs exist. We should be asking how we can work to make these jobs less necessary for the material sustenance of individual people such that they could work in ways that actually produce a tangible benefit that serves the common good.

Berry has a proposal in his essay "The Hidden Wound" for how this might be done. The pivotal question is what the product of the work is. And by this standard, much blue-collar and white-collar work is simply bad work.

> What would be a just wage for a life of carrying off other people's cans and bottles? A million dollars a year would not be enough, because such a job can be performed only by the forfeiture of the effective life of the spirit in this world. Such work is not, in the usual sense, an accomplishment. It is not productive work. The only conceivable standard for it is quantitative; it can be done thoroughly or not; one can haul off either all the cans and bottles or only some of them. It is work that by its nature cannot be good work; though it can be done carefully, it cannot be well done. There is no art in it, no science, and no skill. Its only virtue is in its necessity.[12]

But this is not an exercise in belittling blue-collar workers or service sector workers. It is, rather, a complaint about the circumstances of our work. Given that, Berry's words for the executives and administrators are far more severe:

> The executive deals in large quantities of products which, typically, are purchased as cheaply as possible, and sold as dearly as possible. Typically, the products are never touched by the executive, and they come from and go to people and places the executive does not know, or care about, or give any respect or allegiance to. Many of those products are not necessary.

Many of them are overpriced. Many of them cause environmental or social or cultural damage. Many of them are destroyed quickly in use but remain indestructible as garbage or pollutants. . . .

The work of the executive is thus as unproductive and as spiritually desolate as that of the garbage collector. Indeed, depending on the toxicity and persistence of the products and by-products, it may be more so. Certainly, by any standard, to haul garbage away is more virtuous than to manufacture it.[13]

What is to be done? The answer has many aspects. To begin, if we come to recognize the membership and to see ourselves as part of it, then the next step is to creatively consider ways we can work to sustain its life. Can you make your home or neighborhood more beautiful through art or horticulture? That is good work. Can you create stronger bonds of affection between church members by hosting groups for communal dinners, Bible studies, or game nights? That is good work. Can you, through your blending of skill, affection, and knowledge, create things that are useful or beautiful? That is very good work. Viewed this way the possibilities before us are endless and exciting.

But there is another answer to the question. The economy that values work that does not promote the health and life of local places must be torn to the ground with all possible speed. Much of our rebellion against this regime will necessarily be indirect. We can opt out of the consumer frenzies that are Black Friday and Amazon Prime Day, to say nothing of the broader Christmas shopping season that so frequently diminishes the celebration of Christ's arrival in the world by distracting us from the beauty of the world. When we must participate in such an economy, we should rebel in the small ways made available to us. Tip service workers generously. Choose carefully what businesses to support, and accept that sometimes you will have to choose the less bad option in the absence of any genuinely good choices. Cultivate the virtues of thrift and handiness, both of which will make you less dependent on habits of mindless consumption.

Finally, we should recognize that ultimately the factory must be stopped, and this will mean dramatic, life-changing action. The activist Mario Savio memorably encouraged his audience in 1964 to "put your bodies upon the gears, and upon the wheels, and upon the levers, and upon all the apparatus, and you've got to make it stop! You've got to indicate to the people who run it, to the people who own it, that unless you're free the machine will be prevented from working at all!"[14]

Throwing our bodies on the gears does not mean engaging in acts of radical violence. In the first place, the simplest reading of Scripture suggests that private individuals should not take up the sword in this way. In the second place, violence tends to beget violence. The person who rises up violently in the cause of justice often rises up violently to support injustice. Rather, to throw our bodies upon the gears is to consistently refuse to participate in the life of the factory. It is to take up alternative liturgies and better work. In dire cases, it means participating in non-violent civil disobedience—sit-ins, boycotts, marches, and the like. But the purpose of disrupting the factory must never be forgotten. The goal is not disruption for disruption's sake. The goal is to embody in our living and our working a better vision of life, to direct people's eyes to the beauty of the world, of human community, and, above all, the beauty of God himself, who in the perfect act of love gave up his body for the liberation of the world.

PART FOUR

THE

PROMISE

OF

COMMUNITY

IN THE EARLY FIFTH CENTURY AD, a young Christian monk came to the city of Rome from somewhere in what is now Turkey. His name was Telemachus. While he was there, the monk went to a stadium to witness the gladiator games.

Struck by the gruesome violence he found there, Telemachus climbed down from the seats and onto the floor of the arena with the gladiators. He implored the men in the name of Jesus to stop fighting. The crowd, enraged at having their entertainment disrupted, was furious. They gathered stones. Moments later Telemachus was dead.

Decadent societies do not like to be called to repentance. Churches who have lost their first love don't much like it either. Yet this is the work set before us. The gospel message remains the same—repentance is the necessary first step toward health and knowing God. But the

Scriptures are full of examples of God using his people to call people to repentance, and more often than not the audience does not listen. Indeed, they often respond with hostility and even violence. So what hope is there for those who cling to a crucified King and call a wandering world to faith?

There are two answers to this question. First, there is the simple hope that flows naturally out of the Spirit-enlightened heart upon hearing the gospel presented. The good news of the gospel is *really* good news—not just about some future state of bliss but about the state of our world today. The Scriptures refer to God as the desire of the nations. They say that someday he will heal the nations. Proverbs tells us that the whole city rejoices when the righteous prosper. It should not surprise us that blessing routinely comes when created beings hear and respond to the call of their Creator.

When we hear a remarkable piece of music or see a beautiful work of art or simply eat a delicious meal, we naturally share that with people because we know it is good, and we are confident others will see its goodness and respond as we did. This should be no less true when talking about the gospel. If we are convinced of its goodness, then we should be confident as we proclaim it to others. Early in the musical *Hamilton* there's a line when a group of young friends meet in a bar. They sing, "Raise a glass to the four of us / tomorrow there'll be more of us." They could sing that because they were confident in the basic truth of their cause and believed the truth would reach others. When you stand in truth, you stand with hope, confidence, and boldness. These characteristics should define us as Christians. So first we recognize that the Christian message tells us the truth about ourselves as individuals and about the nature of our life together with our neighbors.

Second, Christians can hope because the God who made and sustains the world has spoken, has entered the world, has conquered sin and death, and will one day return, bringing heaven down to earth with him. Thus, though our faith is inescapably political and will shape our local communities, our hope is not in any of the cities of today but in the city that is to come, descending from heaven with Christ at his triumphant return when all of creation is brought fully under his rule.

In this final section, then, we must consider the promise of community in two parts. First, the nature of the Christian commonwealth and how Christian societies emerge. Second, the coming advent of the eternal city, a place where there are no more tears or sickness or sadness. And as we consider how to be faithful citizens of that city, we can find real grounds for hope as we are citizens of our earthly cities.

NINE

POLITICAL DOCTRINE
AND CIVIL VIRTUE

In the buildup to the 2012 presidential election, President Obama's campaign released an advertisement built around a fictitious character named Julia. The campaign showed how Julia's life is enriched at various points by the presence of an active government capable of offering valuable social services—HeadStart when she is a child, Pell grants to help finance college, free contraceptives in her twenties as she is starting her career, government-backed loans to help her start a business, and, finally, government-provided health care for her senior years. It's a compelling, idyllic picture of how governments can help individual people through life. But what is most noticeable about the campaign is actually not what is included in it but what is not.

In a column for the *New York Times*, Ross Douthat noted that this vision of life is actually quite lonely and isolated and even paternalistic:

> She seems to have no meaningful relationships apart from her bond with the Obama White House: no friends or siblings or extended family, no husband ("Julia decides to have a child," is all the slide show says), a son who disappears once school starts and parents who only matter because Obamacare grants her the privilege of staying on their health care plan until she's 26. This lends the whole production a curiously patriarchal quality, with Obama as a beneficent Daddy Warbucks and Mitt Romney and Paul Ryan co-starring as the wicked uncles threatening to steal Julia's inheritance.[1]

This vision of human life, which is an increasingly common one among American Democrats, leaves very little room for nongovernmental forms of community. Of course, the Republican vision is seldom much better. During the same campaign that saw Obama release the Julia ad, Republican candidate Mitt Romney said that 47 percent of Americans— those who do not pay income tax because they do not earn enough annual income—will never "take personal responsibility and care for their lives."[2] Though the 2016 campaign is seen by many as a watershed in American politics, the seeds of 2016 were there in 2012. The Democratic campaign had little use for nongovernmental community and the Republican campaign actively despised nearly half the population and virtually every poor American.

We should not be surprised to find that a nation with these competing political visions is unhealthy and mistrusting of one another. But what is the alternative? It cannot be a bland centrism that simply tries to appropriate the least bad aspects of both bankrupt visions. Rather, it must be a genuinely alternative political vision that provides a true vision of life together and also defines the appropriate role that the state should play in facilitating that life. Because Christianity is a true account of reality and not simply a set of vague moral terms that help private individuals, Christianity can provide us with that account. But doing so is difficult and complex, not least because it requires us adopting ways of thinking that have become quite foreign to us in an era in which both parties are so stridently committed to their own bankrupt ideas. That being said, if we begin by defining the big-picture doctrines that shape our political lives, we can create enough common ground that there is room for debate and discussion around particular political principles. So the first step to defining a Christian vision of political life is to define some basic terms.

DISTINGUISHING BETWEEN DOCTRINE AND POLICY

It is possible for two people to agree on doctrine and disagree on a particular policy as it relates to that doctrine. Valuing life is doctrine. A nationwide ban on abortion is policy. Similarly, the idea that just societies should protect and provide for the poor is doctrine. That the government will finance health care for all through a single-payer plan is policy.

The reason much recent Christian political activism in the United States has offered such disappointing returns is that, for the past thirty years (at least), American Christians have obsessed over policy, mostly passed over doctrine with a shrug, and pursued the civil formation of Christian citizens only in a stop-start, halting manner.

Put another way, the political priorities of many American Christians in recent years have been precisely backward. We *ought* to have begun with doctrine because doctrine defines the good life as it relates to political systems and societies. Then we ought to have turned to the formation of citizens. We should have asked what kind of virtues are necessary to live well in community with one another *and* what particular virtues are necessary for responsible political action. Then we should have asked how to cultivate those virtues within our people. Finally, only after attending to these issues, we should have moved on to debating policy, which is how we define the role that the state as an institution plays in our life together alongside a number of other social bodies—families, neighborhoods, businesses, churches, philanthropic organizations, and so on. American Christians, and evangelicals especially, have done the exact opposite. We have focused our energies on policy matters—policies on abortion, policies on marriage, policies on religious liberty. But the underlying doctrine that contextualizes the policies within a broader understanding of the purpose and responsibilities of the state is largely absent or underdeveloped.

Meanwhile, many of the evangelical programs intended to promote civic responsibility in Christian young people have been heavily influenced by the worldview movement (more on this in a moment), such that they often end up equipping students with rehearsed answers to questions no one is asking while mostly neglecting the character and spiritual questions inherent in the work of good citizenship.

The reasons for these failures are not difficult to discern. Policies are relatively simple, and the actions we take to support a policy are obvious. We vote for a policy. We vote for politicians who will vote for policies. The end. Doctrine and formation are both harder, and require far more of us.

CHRISTIAN POLITICAL DOCTRINE

There are three key doctrines that Christians must recover in order to think well about politics on a basic, theoretical level: solidarity, sphere sovereignty, and subsidiarity. Each of these flow from the more fundamental Christian teachings we have already discussed—that people are made in the divine image and placed within a natural order that they have a responsibility to nurture and steward toward the glory of God and flourishing of life. These three political doctrines are attempts to define what that looks like when we turn our attention toward politics.

Solidarity is a sense of shared membership with another person. We use the term jokingly sometimes, as when new parents exchange stories about not sleeping or express sympathy for the rude remark a stranger made at the grocery store. But the concept is both rich and essential. It recognizes that human beings do not exist primarily alone but in community.

We enter the world a member of a community, at least a community with our mother and hopefully with a father too, perhaps siblings as well. But the community with our parents extends outward as well. Simply by virtue of being born, we are tied to our grandparents, aunts, uncles, and cousins. All of these people share some sense of identity with us, and there is nothing we do to create that. It is there naturally. Life goes better for us when we share common purposes, hopes, and goals with the people who are closest to us, either relationally or physically.

But there is an explicitly Christian dimension to solidarity as well. The Bible tells us that all people are sinful themselves and subject to the curse of sin. This, of course, agrees with something we can see naturally: All of us are capable of doing horrific things and are also subject to the pain that is caused by another person's evil behavior. But this insight has a leveling effect. We see it in the Gospels when the religious leaders bring a woman to Jesus who was caught in adultery. Jesus asks for the person who is without sin to cast the first stone. No one can. There is a humility in this realization that leads toward natural feelings of kinship with our fellow human beings. But the Christian argument for solidarity does not end with sin. Christianity also teaches us that all people are made for the same end. So we are not only subject to the same pains, we ultimately are made for the same pleasure and fulfillment—the joy of knowing and loving God.

Once we understand solidarity, an important part of our political doctrine snaps into place. Solidarity gives us a way of thinking about politics that foregrounds peace as a political goal by rejecting the anti-social assumptions of modernism. The modernist understanding of politics thinks the chief good that politics secures for people is sovereignty, which is simply another way of saying the right to narrate one's own identity, to create it over the course of one's life through meaningful action and choice. Yet this ends up meaning that we are all isolated individuals competing with one another to define ourselves. Sovereignty is the way we mediate the conflicts that inevitably arise when millions of self-interested people are locked on the same planet and have to figure out how to self-actualize without killing each other.

One way sovereignty works in practice is through property rights. Recall that Locke's theory is that we have sole ownership of our own body, and when we work, the things our work produces now become *ours* in the same way that our body is. This gives us a way to recognize what is *mine* and what is not, but in time it also dooms us toward all the dangers of a Darwinian-style free-market society.

Another way to make sovereignty work in practice is for all the individual sovereigns to be ruled over by one great sovereign, who mediates disputes. In his book *Before Church and State*, Andrew Willard Jones describes this theory of sovereignty: "Humankind is in a state of constant warfare, everyone against everyone. The sovereign power of the State is a violence so profound and so predictable in its application that everyone submits."[3] Picture two siblings fighting in the living room. The volume is escalating. Unkind words are said. Someone is about to push the other. Then a parent steps into the room. Crisis averted. Why? Because when two smaller parties are threatening violence against each other, a non-violent outcome can be secured when a more powerful party comes along and says, "Knock it off." So that is the modernist theory—human beings are constantly on the brink of killing each other, and it is only the threat of force that keeps the conflict from boiling over.

Solidarity helps us see that there is another possibility. Sovereignty is not the greatest political good. Peace is. But what of peace? We often think of peace in relatively banal terms as simply being the absence of conflict. It is not less than that, of course. We are instructed many times in Scripture to work for precisely that sort of peace. In Romans 12 Paul tells his readers, "If it is possible, as far as it depends on you, live at peace with everyone." Similarly Peter spends much of 1 Peter 2–3 telling his readers to live according to the laws and norms of their position in society, even when that is difficult. He concludes the section by saying, "they must seek peace and pursue it." The author to the Hebrews sounds a similar note in chapter 12 of that epistle when he says, "live in peace with everyone." The idea these authors share is that Christians should not be the ones to produce discord in society but should do everything in their power to live peaceably with their neighbors, even at great cost to themselves.

But we can say more about peace. To understand it purely in negative terms as "the absence of conflict" is to miss the bigger picture. This absence of conflict is meant to produce something. Tim Keller describes it well when he writes of the Hebrew concept of shalom, a word we find often in the Old Testament.

> The world is not like a lava cone, the product of powerful random eruptions, but rather like a fabric. Woven cloth consists of innumerable threads interlaced with one another. Even more than the architectural image, the fabric metaphor conveys the importance of relationship. If you throw thousands of pieces of thread onto a table, no fabric results. The threads must be rightly and intimately related to one another in literally a million ways. Each thread must go over, under, around, and through the others at thousands of points. Only then do you get a fabric that is beautiful and strong, that covers, fits, holds, shelters, and delights. God created all things to be in a beautiful, harmonious, interdependent, knitted, webbed relationship to one another. Just as rightly related physical elements form a cosmos or a tapestry, so rightly related human beings form a community. This interwovenness is what the Bible calls shalom, or harmonious peace.[4]

Thus we pursue social peace because it is in fact the natural state of affairs in creation. It is how the world is meant to work: it is a seamless tapestry, composed of many millions of threads that come together to create a single beautiful thing, all existing in praise to God. We are not, first and foremost, detached autonomous beings defining our own identities; we are, rather, members existing in an interlocking web of life meant to promote the health and happiness of the entire creation.

The second idea we need to recover is one popularized by Dutch theologian and politician Abraham Kuyper called *sphere sovereignty*. Sphere sovereignty helps us make distinctions between the work of different communities that exist in a society. Solidarity tells us that we are united around a common goal, to promote peace, and a common end, to know and love God. Sphere sovereignty helps us see how this works out in practice, since different people and different communities have different responsibilities within the peaceful society. The family is not the church. The church is not the marketplace. The marketplace is not the neighborhood. All of these separate subgroupings within a state or nation fulfill different work to promote the peace of the society.

David Koyzis explains the idea well in his book *Political Visions and Illusions*: "The family, the school, business, labor, the arts and so forth, are all sovereign in their respective spheres. These multiple communities and enterprises possess authority within a specific sphere whose limits are set by the Creator. These limits may not be transgressed without doing harm to the structure of society as ordained by God."[5]

In other words, distinct spheres of society exist with distinct responsibilities to promote the peace of the community. Business owners provide jobs for some and a good or service for others. But it is not their job to provide a formal education to children or to preside over the Lord's Supper or to stand in the pulpit and preach. Their job is to treat their employees well, offer a good wage, and to assist their customers through the creation of a good product. When business moves beyond these responsibilities, abuse inevitably follows. Factory towns built around a single business failed and left thousands destitute. When businesses come into schools, the inevitable response is the cheapening of education as students are not given a proper humane education and are instead shaped toward the desired ends of the business or corporation bankrolling the school. Similar problems arise when churches claim for themselves the responsibilities of the family. Distinct institutions have distinct roles within the healthy society. Indeed, all of the responsibilities of the distinct spheres are better understood as subresponsibilities, for all of them ultimately relate to the promotion and preservation of peace and the work of aiding our neighbor in their sojourn toward Christ.

A particular strength of sphere sovereignty is that it resists the signature errors of both the medieval and the modern eras by resisting attempts to turn society into a strict hierarchy in which one particular human institution presides over all the rest. In the medieval world, that institution was understood to be the church, and the result was a litany of failures and shortcomings that not only destabilized Europe but also confused many as to the nature of the Christian gospel. That said, under modernity we have replaced a pervasive church with a pervasive state that claims sole authority over the public sphere. Thus claims, like those of former Massachusetts congressman Barney Frank who once said that "government is simply another word for things we do together." By placing the many different social spheres alongside each other on a common plain, the sphere sovereignty doctrine helps to properly fence in the authority of both the institutional church and the state, placing both of them under the authority of God.

Finally, the third doctrine we need to keep in mind is that of *subsidiarity*. Though traditionally associated with Roman Catholic social teaching, there is much in the doctrine that Protestants would do well to adopt. Subsidiarity means that when a social problem arises, the body that should address it is the smallest, most local body possible. If a problem can be solved by a household, it should. If a household can't but a neighborhood can, then the neighborhood should. The progression simply continues on upward until you get to the largest social institution, which is usually the state.

Subsidiarity allows us to delegate social responsibility effectively. School systems can be maintained by small towns and cities. The care of children can be provided for by families. Larger problems, on the other hand, require larger institutions to address. A national highway system can't reasonably be maintained by a private business or a city. You need a large national government for that. Similar concerns apply to the military. Many Western countries have concluded the same about health care, arguing that due to the expense of modern medicine and the complexities of providing care for a large population, it makes sense for the national government to oversee health care.

The example of health care speaks to one of the particular strengths of the principle of subsidiarity. Unlike right-wing attempts to absolutize the idea of "small government" as a political goal, subsidiarity shifts the discussion in a helpful direction by arguing that government should do only what government is large enough to do and no more. So allegedly "big government" projects, such as a single-payer health care system, could be argued for without making the more left-wing error of ignoring all nonstate forms of human community. At its best, subsidiarity helps us to recognize the unique social utility offered by different human institutions and frees up those communities to do what they are best at.

Taken together, this sketch of a Christian doctrine of politics tells us that human society exists to aid men and women in their calling to know and love God, that the chief good political societies can realize together is peace, that different subgroups within a society have different things to do to serve society, and that each of these subgroups should only attempt to do the things they are most qualified to do. Implicitly, then, this vision of politics assumes a robust interwoven web of communities, all of which are serving one another and the common good of all through working in business, the arts, maintaining a home, serving in government, working in full-time ministry, and so on.

WHERE DO GOOD CITIZENS COME FROM?

In a letter written to the Massachusetts militia in 1798, president John Adams wrote, "Our Constitution was made only for a moral and religious People. It is wholly inadequate to the government of any other."[6] Adams meant that ways of living together and organizing society presuppose certain things about people and therefore require certain types of people to function well. We can have great political principles and great policy ideas, but without citizens able to realize those ideas, they won't get us very far. Thus one way of tracing our decline into social breakdown is to ask about what methods and practices we have as a nation for shaping people into humble, wise, responsible citizens.

With this understanding in place, we can now start to ask questions about the formation of Christian citizens. This is an area where the American church has struggled in recent years, for obvious reasons. The ideal Christian citizen is the person who has been humbled by the teaching of the faith, has a rich daily practice of Christian piety, and therefore enters into the work of civil life with confidence and wisdom. But, given what we have already observed about the failures of the church, how would we expect humble, wise citizens to emerge from such communities? The answer is "we can't." Given that, it is worth rehearsing what is meant by a humble citizen and what is meant by a wise citizen, for both of these qualities are essential.

One of the chief themes of the Christian faith as revealed in Scripture is the upside-down nature of Christ's kingdom. Jesus tells his disciples that the first will be last and the last first. He tells them that in order to be great one must be a servant. He says that it is particularly hard for the rich to enter the kingdom of God, and in contrast the kingdom of God belongs to, among others, children, the meek, and the poor in spirit. In many ways, these ideas are radically out of step with much of what is typical public life in America today.

Part of the challenge here is predictable. In a society that believes a person narrates their own identity into existence, it should not surprise us that there are strong incentives to narrate very loudly. The realm of politics particularly affords one the opportunity to do this as it is a place in which one can not only establish one's identity but establish oneself as righteous. But Christians cannot allow themselves to be part of this performative politics.

Of course, one answer as to how this might be done is to default toward an Anabaptist political theology. In this approach, the church is seen as a complete society in itself. Thus our involvement as Christians in the world outside the church is unnecessary and can even become a danger to our faith. In extreme forms, whole sectors of public life are judged to be unsuitable for Christians—the military and government most often. But this is the wrong lesson to take from Christ's words in the Gospels. Indeed, though it is seldom recognized, this approach actually *diminishes* the severity of what Christ said. It confuses a description of the sort of spirit that should define the Christian to a simple list of jobs or occupations forbidden to Christians.

The argument of the Gospels is that the kingdom belongs to the poor in spirit. Certainly, material riches can hinder us from acquiring this spirit. But when we consider the broader testimony of Scripture, we see that, though it is difficult, there are rich people in the kingdom of heaven. There are, likewise, government officials in the kingdom and even soldiers and military. When the Roman official Jairus came to Jesus, Jesus never told him to leave his position. When soldiers came to John the Baptist, he did not tell them to lay down their swords. When the wealthy merchant Lydia of Thyatira experienced the new birth, Paul's directions to her were not to sell everything she had and give it to the poor. Success, power, and wealth can make it harder for us to love God. But when we have those advantages and love God, the opportunity to steward them for his purposes is great. Indeed, this is precisely what Lydia seems to have done in the book of Acts as she helped finance Paul's work as a missionary.

The vision of the Gospels is not of material poverty and powerlessness per se, but of a spiritual emptying of the self so that we can be filled with the Spirit. It is of a person defined by a love for God and neighbor grounded in gratitude to God that leads to a self-forgetfulness, a constant awareness that what the person has is all given by God and given for a purpose. And the purpose is not the exaltation of the individual recipient. God gives us good gifts, and we are called, through the skill and knowledge that is *also* a gift from God, to multiply that gift, to expand it, and to give it away for the good of all.

The example of Jean Valjean, the protagonist in Victor Hugo's *Les Misérables*, is instructive here. At one point in the story, Valjean is the mayor of a small French town where he also runs a factory that provides jobs for a number of people in the village. Valjean is a picture of power and ingenuity, all under control and directed outward from the self and toward his neighbor in hopes of advancing their good. He lives simply, doesn't spend much money, takes a far smaller salary than could be justified given his importance to the business, and uses his considerable intelligence to serve the people he employs. Andy Crouch explains the idea well in his book *Playing God* as he describes the sort of leader who is largely indifferent to their own agenda and makes themselves and their abilities available to others: "[The spiritual disciplines] make us a people who have a holy indifference to worldly power and a passionate commitment to using the power we have been given, which is everything we need and more, to restore the image of God in the world."[7]

This raises an obvious question. People who are committed to pursuing the lower place, who lay aside their own needs to serve others, people who give themselves away, can't they be taken advantage of? And if so, isn't that a significant risk with carrying a humble spirit into the halls of power? Surely in a place like that a bit of elbow-throwing is warranted? But this is not an option Christ leaves open to us in the Gospels. John Calvin explains why in his commentary on the Sermon on the Mount.

> When Christ promises to such persons the inheritance of the earth, we might think it exceedingly foolish. Those who warmly repel any attacks, and whose hand is ever ready to revenge injuries, are rather the persons who claim for themselves the dominion of the earth. And experience certainly shows that, the more mildly their wickedness is endured, the more bold and insolent does it become. Hence arises the diabolical proverb, that "We must howl with the wolves, because the wolves will immediately devour every one who makes himself a sheep." But Christ places his own protection, and that of the Father, in contrast with the fury and violence of wicked men, and declares, on good grounds, that the meek will be the lords and heirs of the earth. The children of this world never think themselves safe, but when they fiercely revenge the injuries that are done them, and defend their life by the "weapons of war," (Ezekiel 32:27). But as we must believe, that Christ alone is the guardian of our life, all that remains for us is to "hide ourselves under the shadow of his wings," (Psalms 17:8). We must be sheep, if we wish to be reckoned a part of his flock.[8]

The dilemma Calvin is describing is a familiar one. Will you get your hands dirty in order to advance the good? That is the point of the proverb Calvin cites—the only way to avoid getting devoured by a wolf is to act like a wolf. In a political atmosphere as fractious as our own, there is a powerful temptation toward precisely this approach. It explains why both right and left have become more entrenched, angry, and mistrusting of the other. They both see the worst in each other (with reason) and have become convinced that the only way anything can be accomplished is through force and trickery. But note how Calvin responds: he sees that this is a shell game. The wicked who grasp at power, taking whatever they can reach and constantly scanning the room for stepladders to extend their reach, are not secure. "They never think themselves safe." Such a life is a constant balancing act, like a man on the deck of a rocking ship. But, Calvin goes on, the Christian believer is not like this. Because he or she believes that Christ is the guardian of life, "all that remains for us is to 'hide ourselves under the shadow of his wings.'"[9] In 2016 evangelicals made the choice to dress as a wolf. Some of Donald Trump's endorsers have been quite plain about this. Jerry Falwell Jr. has said on more than one occasion that Christians do not need a pastor-in-chief or a nice guy in the Oval Office. They need a "street fighter."[10]

But this is idolatry. It tells the sheep that the only way they can be safe is to dress as wolves. Implicitly, it tells the sheep that the Shepherd is not in control, is not attending to their needs. The first virtue every Christian who aspires to responsible citizenship must take up is humility and its companion, which is a humble reliance on God to take our meager loaves and fish and turn them to something greater.

The second virtue we must take up is wisdom. To understand what this means, we should contrast Christian wisdom with another *w* word that has been fashionable in Christian circles for some time: *worldview*. The worldview movement sought to help Christian young people develop a framework for understanding the world by defining various schools of thought that offer a comprehensive account of reality. Thus there was a "Christian" worldview, a "materialist" worldview, a "Muslim" worldview, and so on. The approach is not altogether wrong, of course. Ideas do, as the saying goes, have consequences. But the worldview movement far too often attempted to distill worldviews down to little more than a set of intellectual aphorisms that all held together and never developed in unpredictable or inconsistent ways.

The result for Christian young people is that far too often they did not learn to think for themselves, to take basic Christian principles and translate those into their particular circumstances. Rather, they memorized rote answers to predefined problems. Lacking the ability to reason for themselves, they were left utterly unprepared for even the straightforward work of Christian evangelization and catechesis, let alone the more complicated work of judicious Christian citizenship. Alissa Wilkinson described the problem well, writing, "A worldview framework that can help us identify false ideas can quickly become a categorize-and-dismiss system—an easy way for us to put our 'opponent' in a box and ignore what they have to say, all in the name of 'loving them.' Then we can even joke about them or sneer at them."[11]

How does Christian wisdom differ from worldview? Christian wisdom does not begin with predefined categories and questions and answers. It does not begin with simple boxes into which people can easily be sorted. Rather, Christian wisdom begins with a careful consideration of reality. It enters the world confidently, expecting that whatever it finds will be interesting and will show us a bit more about who God is. The folk songwriter Joe Pug once used the phrase, "I have come to be untroubled in my seeking."[12] That is the spirit of Christian wisdom. It is at rest, trusting in the truthfulness of God and the integrity of his creation. On the website of the Davenant Institute, a nonprofit I serve with, wisdom is described like this:

> Wisdom is a gathering of truth in love of God, so as to embody and radiate it to the world. It comes from possessing the principles of reality in the mind, illuminated by the Spirit-filled heart, and for the sake of the knowledge of God and glorifying Him. It makes free men and women capable of prudence and virtuous practice who can lead in their communities as servant heroes.[13]

How do we acquire wisdom? To begin, wisdom requires patience. Wisdom is not acquired by simply reading the books of a favorite

Christian author. Wisdom is cultivated over time through careful reading, conversation, and a steady, slow following of Christ in the stuff of daily life. It is the result of regular habits of receptivity by which we open ourselves up to the instruction of God as he offers it to us in Scripture and in nature.

Equipped with this wisdom and characterized by humility, Christians can be a powerful force for good in the life of their community.

WHAT OF POLICY?

In a nation obsessed with the fierce debates over particular policy questions, reflections on political doctrine and civil virtue can seem boring, remote. "But what do you think about health care?" you might find yourself impatiently asking. And certainly some policy matters are clear-cut. Throughout our nation's history there have been countless instances of clearly racist policies that have no justification in Christianity—slavery, Jim Crow, redlining, mass incarceration. All of these are practices that have been based in some fashion in political policies. In every case, Christians ought to have condemned the government policies that allowed them. And time after time white Christians have been fearful of condemning these policies. Though you cannot solve for human evil through policy, you can use policy to condemn and punish evil. Far too often Christians have been reluctant to do this on questions of racial justice.

There are also cases where there may be *some* ambiguity on general principles for the Christian, but where the on-the-ground policy proposals are still relatively clear-cut. For example, there is some debate among Christian theologians about whether it is moral to charge interest for a loan. Some have argued that interest payments are actually a form of theft, because they are extracting wealth from another person without offering anything in exchange. The debate is tricky because it raises real questions about how specific Old Testament laws translate into our context. But whatever you may think about the difference between charging no interest and charging low interest rates, there is no argument whatever for allowing payday loan companies to charge interest at the rates they do. Yet we allow these lending companies, which are little more than loan sharks dressed up in a respectable suit, to exist with minimal challenge from Christians. It would be one thing if the relevant public debate were over charging zero interest or low interest when offering a loan. But in the United States today the most relevant debate is over high interest rates, and on that policy matter the Christian testimony is plain.

Finally, there are cases where a public policy ought to exist but currently does not. Abortion is the most obvious example to cite here. It is the near-unanimous view of Christians throughout history, only being challenged in the last fifty to one hundred years, that abortion is a great evil. Because the law should reflect what is true and just, there should be policies in place that prohibit abortion.

Yet all three of these cases—racism, interest, and abortion—also demonstrate the limitations of policy. Policies that reflect and agree with God's moral law are good and should be supported by Christians. But if our work stops there, the good our political advocacy will accomplish will be far smaller than it ought to be. White supremacy manifests itself in policy, but also in other venues as well. The crisis of trust that now exists between African Americans and the police, for example, can be helped by better policies, but policy alone cannot heal the wounds. Similarly, the questions of poverty that exist along the edges of the payday loan debate cannot be fully addressed by policy. Nor can the issues that run alongside the abortion debate. Policy will not provide loving adoptive homes for the children of mothers who are unable to provide the needed care for their child. We need more than just policy.

This is why both doctrine and virtue are so important. The most basic and proper work of Christian citizenship is to cultivate the virtues of humility and wisdom in order to make oneself a gifted public servant in whatever venue God has called one to. By understanding the basic Christian political doctrines as well as the civil virtues, we can equip ourselves to repair the fracturing body politic of America and to offer a positive vision of mutual flourishing and hope in our decadent society.

TEN

THE ETERNAL CITY

PROFESSOR JERRAM BARRS ONCE TOLD THE STORY of a conversation he had with a child at his church about heaven. The child's parents had been reading to him from C. S. Lewis's Chronicles of Narnia and the child had come to a conclusion that bothered him a bit. In a frank conversation with Barrs, the child said that "I don't really want to go to heaven when I die. I want to go to Narnia!" Barrs could only ruefully smile and tell the child that if heaven was like what many Christians think it will be, he feels the same way.

We can see how the child would end up there, of course. If, as the popular evangelical story about the end of the world would have it, God is going to burn everything up and make a brand-new heaven and earth at the end of all things, what exactly is the point of living and working in the world? At best, our life in this world is simply an opportunity to tell people about God, the gospel, heaven, and hell. But there isn't really a significance or enduring meaning to the physical creation that extends beyond that. Pushed toward its natural conclusion, we end up with something like this: "For those in the marketplace, work exists to finance your life and the ministry of a church and parachurch ministries so that they can evangelize others and pile them into the lifeboat that is going to escape this burning-down wreck of a world. For those in full-time ministry, your work is to do the evangelizing."

This, quite naturally, leads to all sorts of questions. If I make the same money whether I work well or work poorly, does it matter? Thoughtful Christians might respond by proof texting their way to an answer that says working well is a good in itself, but the logic of their position would tend in the other direction. Indeed, I once heard a friend put it as starkly as I can imagine: ultimately it doesn't matter how well you do your work. In fact, you should aspire to work as little as possible to provide a minimal level of material security for your family so you can give as much of your time as possible to prayer and as much of your money as possible to the church. Fortunately for those of us who feel intuitively uncomfortable with such a response, the good news is that, well, *that* isn't the good news.

The fear behind the child's question is that ultimately the things we love in this world won't last and in one sense don't even really matter all that much. They're good for fleeting pleasures and not much else. The child in this story is essentially being given a life of melancholic asceticism and told that that is what Christianity is. Yet something inside him rebels against that. It seems to cheapen the world as it exists around us and reduces our life today to an extended waiting until we can be emancipated from fleshly existence. He likes Narnia better than what he thinks heaven will be like, and he's not sure what to do with that.

GOD ISN'T GOING TO DESTROY THE WORLD

Why do evangelicals think that God is going to destroy his good creation? What is the source of the tiresome jokes about how our material life in this world doesn't *really* matter because "it's all going to burn anyway"?

The confusion often begins with 2 Peter 3:10, a verse that has been widely misunderstood to suggest that God will burn the cosmos with fire at the *eschaton* before creating the "new heavens and new earth" described in Revelation. The text from Peter in the RSV says, "The day of the Lord will come like a thief, and then the heavens will pass away with a loud noise, and the elements will be dissolved with fire, and the earth and the works that are upon it will be burned up." It sounds open and shut, certainly, but we should pause before considering the text itself and note something about the biblical account.

In the first place, it is striking that much of the biblical language describing God's act of rescuing humans and creation uses language not of re-creation but of restoration. For example, in 2 Corinthians 5:17, where Paul refers to

Christians as "new" creations, the word he uses for "new" is *kainos*, which *Strong's Concordance* says refers to something that is "new in quality." This same word, *kainos* is what John uses to describe the "new" heaven and earth in Revelation 21:1. The newness he is describing refers to a quality, rather than to age.

Why is this significant? Because the Greek language also has the word *neos*, which refers to something that is "new with respect to age." This is the word the New Testament authors often use when describing something that is young. For example, when Jesus is speaking to Peter in John 21 and says that Peter did certain things when he was "younger," the word used there is *neos*. The same is true in Acts 5:6 where we read of the "young" men taking away the bodies of Ananias and Sapphira after they had lied to Peter about the gift they were giving the church. Though both of these words, *kainos* and *neos* are often rendered as "new" in English, they have different meanings.

If Revelation 21 was describing the actual from-scratch creation of a new heaven and new earth, wholly distinct from the earth we live on today, we would expect to see the word *neos* being used. But that is not what we find. When the Bible talks about the newness resulting from salvation, whether we are speaking of people as in 2 Corinthians 5 or the cosmos as in Revelation 21, the text is talking about a new quality, something that is being renewed through the emergence of new characteristics. It is not speaking of an entirely new thing.

The language the Bible uses elsewhere further underscores this point. Reconciliation, a common biblical image for salvation, means being restored to a once-lost relationship. Redemption refers to regaining one's freedom after losing it. It means being bought *back* and restored to a previous state.

Dutch Reformed theologian Al Wolters makes the point in his book *Creation Regained* where he writes, "It is quite striking that virtually all of the basic words describing salvation in the Bible imply a *return* to an originally good state or situation."[1] In one of his more arresting passages Paul describes creation itself as "groaning" under the burden of sin, longing to be set free from it. But this would be odd indeed if it is only set free through an act of destruction.

Of course, those considerations only help us with the broader biblical themes. They don't help us with 2 Peter 3, or at least not directly. But Wolters is helpful here as well. In *Creation Regained*, Wolters notes that the key Greek word that modern translations render as "will be burned up" is actually not the Greek term found in nearly all of the oldest and most reliable manuscripts. The word that the biblical author uses would be better rendered as "will be found." Wolters then notes that the NIV actually translates Peter as saying that the works "will be laid bare." But this, of course, is quite a different meaning. If a thing is found or laid bare, that thing obviously still exists.

Moreover, the internal logic of Peter's text supports this alternative reading of 2 Peter 3:10. Prior to this verse, Peter has been setting up what he is saying here by likening the coming judgment to the judgment that God visited on the earth in the Genesis flood. Peter even says that the earth "was destroyed" in the flood. But, of course, *destroyed* there does not refer to an annihilation or obliteration. God does not recreate the world from nothing for a second time after the flood. Rather, the flood is a purifying judgment of that which was harming God's creation. Thus Wolters writes, "The day of the Lord will bring the fires of judgment and a cataclysmic convulsion of all creation, but what emerges from the crucible will be 'a new heaven and a new earth, the home of righteousness,' and it is presumably there that 'the earth and the works that are upon it will be found,' now purified from the filth and perversion of sin."[2] The image, then, is of the heavens and earth passing through a blacksmith's fire, being heated so as to remove the impurities and the pure metal can be seen more clearly and shine forth in its true beauty.

This reading of Peter not only makes better sense of the rest of Scripture and the rest of what Peter says in chapter 3, it even echoes the way that Paul and Jude speak of fire purifying individual Christians. Understood this way, Scripture is teaching that both humanity and the physical creation will be saved by passing through fire, and what comes through on the other side of the burning will be renewed, purified of sin, but still recognizably itself. We will still have bodies that can be recognized and the earth itself will presumably still be recognizable to us.

This is why in Revelation the eternal city is described as descending *to* the earth. We are not taken out of creation and brought into heaven; heaven, the realm where God dwells, comes down to earth as God comes to dwell with his people. As the great Robert Farrar Capon put it, the road to heaven does not run *from* the earth, but through it.[3]

This explains why we can be hopeful about the world. We hope for the world because we know that God loves it. As an old pastor of mine liked to say, "God doesn't create junk, and he doesn't junk what he creates." And that is a hopeful thing to consider, particularly in an era of climate change.

THE ETERNAL CITY

So, what is this eternal city like? If we hope because the coming of this city is as certain as the goodness and mercy of God, well, what should we expect from this city to come? Revelation 21:24 answers the question: "The nations of them which are saved shall walk in the light of [that city]: and the kings of the earth do bring their glory and honor into it" (KJV). Two things are worth noting in this text.

First, note that it speaks of the "*nations* of them which are saved." One of the reasons we wince at the conventional evangelical picture of the afterlife is that we imagine ourselves stripped bare of all the things that are distinctive about ourselves, all the qualities that God seemingly placed in us but seem to disappear as we float about ethereally in the heavens. But this text rebuts that picture of the afterlife. The eternal city descends to earth. And the people who stream into it come as recognizable nations. The text, in fact, suggests a procession of nations, not unlike the opening ceremony of the Olympics, as each nation of those who look on their King with love enter into the joy of his city and bring with them the glories of their nations.

We might imagine the Germans entering with *Ein Feste Burg* on their lips, while the Chinese Christians sing *Father Long Before Creation*, and the Zulus march in joyfully singing *Jesu Nkosi*, which means "Jesus is King." The picture is joyful, exuberant, and unapologetically earthy.

This scene also offers a bracing rebuke to both the American right and American left. Conservatives often speak—sometimes in ways that are explicitly racist—of obviously superior cultures and obviously inferior cultures. And while there may be some limited way in which such language is valid—it's okay to say that a culture that does not practice human sacrifice is in some sense superior to one that does—it can also be used to denigrate cultures that are actually quite beautiful and that, Revelation strongly suggests, will bring that beauty into the eternal city. Similarly, the left can make of "diversity" a jarring and manipulative monoculture that denigrates all difference and distinction. It can see cultural differences as being innately dangerous and therefore as something to be muted and suppressed to avoid creating controversy or conflict. But, again, the Scriptures suggest this is wrongheaded. One nation does not look like another, and yet Scripture seems to suggest that we come into the eternal city as members of recognizable (and presumably distinct) nations. One need not be a racist, in other words, to recognize that there is something beautiful about the distinctiveness and exclusivity of cultures and people groups.

Revelation also says that the kings of the earth will bring "their glory" into the eternal city. What does that mean? Well, in 1 Corinthians 11:7 Paul says that man is "the image and glory of God" and further that "woman is the glory of man." God makes man from the dust and woman is made from man. This would seem to suggest that the "glory" of a thing is that which is made from it. Further, in Psalm 8:5 the psalmist describes humans as being "crowned" with glory and honor, and immediately proceeds to describe the dominion humans have over creation. Thus we might say that the glory of humans refers to the things they have made and the things they have dominion over. So when we speak of the kings of the earth bringing their glory into the eternal city, it is not a stretch to think that this refers to the works of their hands and presumably the works of their nations. So, the good things we create today will, in some sense, be with us in the eternal city.

We should be careful here. The Reformed theologian J. Todd Billings offered a good corrective to this view in a column for *Christianity Today* in which he noted that this sort of thinking can, first, denigrate the work done by the many people who do *not* build cathedrals or write symphonies *and*, more importantly, that it can also lead to a person associating heaven more closely with their vision of the best of all possible worlds rather than focusing on the most important and best thing about heaven: that it is where God dwells. These concerns are quite reasonable. That being said, it is not a hard issue to address.

The point here is not that there is a rarefied class of creative people who create beautiful things that God loves and those things exist forever. The point is that when we behold the One for whom we were made, God himself, we bring with us the things we have made and the things we have done and throw them all at his feet for his glory. So we bring things that are recognizably *ours* into the city and then we give them all back to Christ. This, of course, is resonant with the language of the saints casting their crowns at Christ's feet earlier in Revelation and also overlaps a lot with the teachings of several parables in which Jesus tells the story of a landowner entrusting money to various servants and then having those servants come to him at his return to lay their work before him. The idea is that those who are found in Christ, who receive his righteousness and thus can stand before God, will bring their glory and honor into his eternal city, where they will lay it before him as an act of love and worship. So the cathedral goes on existing. The music too. And all the other many things that God's people have made for the delight of humanity and the glory of God.

This point was driven home for me powerfully one day while I went on a walk in St. Paul, Minnesota, where I had just moved after graduating college. On the drive in to the city I had passed a cathedral and was determined to see it. But I wanted to come to it as people would have come to it in the days of the great cathedrals, not in a car that they then park in a lot across from the church, but on foot, slowly approaching the church from a distance and seeing it grow before you as you come closer. So I walked down Selby Avenue and came to the beginnings of Cathedral Hill. And in the distance I could see the dome of the church rising above the neighborhood. I walked toward the church and then entered through a side door and saw, for the first time, the glorious vault of the Cathedral of Saint Paul. It is, a tour guide told me once, one of the finest churches in North America. A European cardinal once toured it and said it would not be out of place in France among the legendary cathedrals of the Western church. When I first encountered it, I was simply taken by the scale of the thing, its overwhelming size and the way it towered above me as if to say, "You will never be able to take in all of me."

But then as I looked closer I began to see things, things that reminded me that this cathedral is not ultimately gesturing to itself but to the One who is worshiped inside it. I was reminded of this as I entered—the large wooden doors sit beneath a huge stone relief of Christ on the judgment seat. To one side, an angel holds the cross and to the other a torch—both religious and scientific knowledge are held together under his rule. And the peoples of the earth, pictured directly below his throne, live their lives before his face. I passed in, and as I entered the worship space my eyes were drawn upward to a golden dome resting on open windows, such that it appears to be a golden sphere sitting on pure light. This harkens back to the medieval cosmology that saw the realm of God as being the outer reaches of the cosmos, past the seven planets and the empyrean and in a circle reserved for itself where the pure essence of God resided. And so all the beauty of that cathedral is ultimately meant to draw our eyes to the beauty of God.

As I walked out of that cathedral, I went out through the main doors, exiting under the judgment seat, and was quite taken by the view: the cathedral sits on the tallest hill adjacent to downtown and looks out over the whole city, a powerful symbol of the church watching protectively over its flock.

As I stood there I imagined thousands upon thousands of Christians from the Twin Cities streaming up the hill and toward the church to worship God in the world to come. Imagine the site of it—every pew filled. Imagine the sound—thousands of saints singing to their King in a space designed to produce the purest and most beautiful sound possible. The scene is like something out of *Les Misérables*. In the most recent film version, the musical starring Hugh Jackman, Anne Hathaway, Eddie Redmayne, and Russell Crowe in a much maligned role as Javert, as Valjean dies he experiences the beatific vision, being drawn toward God, not only by Fantine but by others who helped lead him to God, most notably the priest Bienvenu, who showed him mercy when he was a thief. And as he passes through the door that will bring him to God, we find the streets of Paris. Some criticized the move, arguing that he should have beheld pure light or something other than the earthly city. And yet if Revelation is true, then the image the film closed on, the departed heroes of the film singing joyously "in the garden of the Lord," which is the city of Paris, is exactly right.

The point of this is that beautiful things unveil themselves to us slowly over time. If we spend two hours staring at Rembrandt's *Prodigal Son*, we will see things we would not have seen with only an hour to view it. This is true of all good things God gives us. The inside is larger than the outside. And this is why a literally endless ocean of time to exist in God's world is such glorious news. Imagine the beauties we will find in the world given a literal eternity to explore it.

Many of us know the experience of delighting in a thing after a sustained time of patient looking at it and thinking about it. I have experienced this myself with the Cathedral of Saint Paul.

Several months after that first encounter with the church, I sat at a bar in downtown Minneapolis with my friend Matt and told him about an idea I had. I'd seen an ad in a local paper for upcoming performances of Handel's *Messiah* performed by the Minnesota State Orchestra held at the Cathedral of Saint Paul. I had recently started dating a girl I'd known in Lincoln but had gotten to know better after we both moved (separately) to the Twin Cities. It was going well—better than I could have ever imagined, in fact. "I can think of worse ways of proposing," said Matt with a grin, "than at a cathedral after a performance of the *Messiah*." And so, buoyed by that conversation, I called the state orchestra the next Monday and bought two tickets. I had to dip into savings to afford them, given my uncertain recently graduated twenty-something financial situation, but I figured that in the worst-case scenario in which Joie and I broke up, I could treat my roommate to a great performance. And in the best case scenario, well, it'd be pretty great.

Three months passed. After two had gone by, I decided to propose. I got a ring from my future mother-in-law that had belonged to Joie's grandmother. Joie had told me about the ring before, and I knew she didn't like the setting. So I took the ring to a jeweler eight days before the concert and worked with them to design a new ring using the same stones. The jeweler asked when I needed the ring. "Well, December 9 would be ideal," I said. That was a little more than a week away. The jeweler was startled. "That's awfully soon." I nodded, explained that the ring had been mailed from Alabama and I had only gotten it the day before. Then I said, "And really the reason I want it in eight days is because I have tickets for us to see the *Messiah* at the Cathedral and I want to surprise her and propose after the performance on the steps of the Cathedral overlooking the city." The jeweler looked at me for a moment. Then he grinned. "We'll have it for you the morning of the ninth."

A week later, the day had arrived. I picked up my dry-cleaned suit in the morning. Then I drove to the jeweler and picked up the ring. I waited a few hours. Then it was time to pick Joie up. She had no idea what I had planned and didn't know how urgent the timing was. We rushed out the door once she was ready, ten minutes late for our reservation at an Italian restaurant down the street on Cathedral Hill from the church. While Joie was in the bathroom, I explained our situation to the server and they got our food out as quickly as possible. We ate a wonderful meal and then walked to the Cathedral. As we walked, the Cathedral growing ever taller before our eyes, I occasionally slipped my hand into my pockets, feeling in one pocket the tickets and in the other the case that held the ring.

As we stood outside the church, which had hundreds of people milling around it, I gave her the tickets. We went in and listened to over two hours of heavenly music—and I mean that quite literally—the sounds of the symphony and the singers rose up into the golden dome of the church and cascaded back down to us. As the show wound down we came to the "Hallelujah Chorus," which famously calls its listeners to rejoice because "the Lord God omnipotent reigneth / and he shall reign forever and ever." We stood, as is the custom, several thousand standing to honor a King that many of those present did not even know. After the show, and after most of the crowd had filtered out, we went outside and stood on the steps, Joie looking up at the relief and me standing behind her, where I dropped to one knee.

She said yes.

FURTHER UP AND FURTHER IN

There are things we experience in this world, physical earthy things, that are beautiful and tell us something about the world to come, things like cathedrals and seventeenth-century oratorios and rings that have been in the family for seventy years and long-standing customs like the groom proposing on one knee, a gesture that suggests vulnerability and fealty and an intention to serve. And there are more things than that—a good family meal where the only thing more pleasant than the food itself is the conversation, the pleasure taken in making something beautiful that we mean to share with someone else, whether that is a painting or a cake or a story.

The good news of the Christian faith is that these things will not fail and that the delight we derive from them today, delight that God smiles upon since he is the giver of the gift, will continue on into eternity, world without end. Christ's promise to his people to come to our rescue and renew both us and the world will not fail, even when the church has been compromised and assailed by enemies both within and without. These things will not fail when the world itself seems to be failing. And they will not fail at the end of all things when God returns and creation is laid bare. And the reason they will not fail is that in their goodness and beauty they reflect the goodness and beauty of the God who is eternal, the God for whom and to whom are all things made.

In the final book of the Chronicles of Narnia, C. S. Lewis describes Lucy, Peter, and Edmund's entry into Aslan's country. He uses the phrase "further up and further in" to describe life in that place:

> About half an hour later—or it might have been half a hundred years later, for time there is not like time here—Lucy stood with her dear friend, her

oldest Narnian friend, the Faun Tumnus, looking down over the wall of that garden, and seeing all Narnia spread out below. But when you looked down you found that this hill was much higher than you had thought: it sank down with shining cliffs, thousands of feet below them and trees in that lower world looked no bigger than grains of green salt. Then she turned inward again and stood with her back to the wall and looked at the garden.

"I see," she said now at last, thoughtfully. "I see now. This garden is like the Stable. It is far bigger inside than it was outside."

"Of course, Daughter of Eve," said the Faun. "The further up and further in you go, the bigger everything gets. The inside is larger than the outside."[4]

The conceit of this book has been that Christianity is good news not only for a dying church that needs to be reminded of its truths, but for a failing world that is itself beset by many evils. And it is good news not because God will snatch us out of this world but because—again I must quote Capon—the road to redemption runs through this world. And as we run it, we realize that this world itself is full of surprises, that the deeper we sink into it and the closer we look at it, the more we see, the larger it becomes. The eternal city, then, is not a place to fear because of its monotony and tedium, but a place to anticipate with joy because it promises that we will never come to the end of its delights, the further into it we go the larger it becomes.

In summer 2010 I stood in the front of a small church in Lincoln, Nebraska. Nearby one of my closest friends stood at the center of the stage next to the pastor with a tear rolling down his cheek. Down the aisle came his fiancée, accompanied by her father. They're a good pair, Matt and Ashley—Mashley, as we referred to them when they were dating and in the puppy dog phase of their relationship, hopelessly and obnoxiously (and, when we cared to admit it, beautifully) smitten with one another. There was a point in the ceremony when Ashley, too excited to contain it, scrunched up her face, arched her shoulders, and laughed, as if her whole body was having to release a bit of excess happiness just so she could make it through the ceremony. The congregation offered their own benediction to this joy in the form of happy laughter.

I'm a naturally cynical person. I have enough humor to hide it when I wish to, but I'm good at looking through things. I'm good at seeing why something isn't as good as it first *seems* to be. Indeed, that little word *seems* may well be one of my favorites. That word is a protection, a way of warding off real belief in order to avoid the inevitable disappointment that follows sincere belief. I'm good at looking behind the curtain to see what's *really* there—and helping others do the same.

But that day reminded me of something important. Sometimes there isn't anything behind the curtain. The reality is what's in front of you, the solid, good, and joyful thing right there hiding in plain sight. There isn't anything to see through. It's all there, plain, whole, and exuberant.

The world supplies us with an infinite range of things that can delight us in that way if we will let them—the safety of a warm family and comfortable home, the song of a nightingale in the trees, the laughter of children, a smoke-filled apartment and friends singing loudly and occasionally off key, the pink sunlight hitting a towering skyscraper at sunset, the pomp and pageantry of weddings.

I suspected after that day that weddings would be the sort of thing that rewards attentiveness. Matt and Ashley's faces during that ceremony, both spilling over with joy in their own ways, helped me see that. A year later I found myself standing in the front of the same auditorium—with all the same guys, in fact—but this time I was the groom. And that idea about weddings was confirmed for me. There is something profound in singing "To Christ the Lord, let every tongue its noblest tribute bring" with 250 people as you stand next to your about-to-be wife.

Last year my five-year-old daughter was in her first wedding. She was a flower girl. And suddenly I found myself moving into the phase of life when I watched my daughter wear a dress and walk the aisle, leaving behind flowers that made a path for her cousin to walk toward her groom. And it was still true—the inside was larger than the outside. Someday I may find myself taking that walk *with* my daughter. And I expect that on that day the same thing will hold.

We are, all of us, implicated in and called to something of the most profound importance. Christianity tells us that weddings are not the only thing in which the inside is larger than the outside. That description, in fact, applies to all of life.

Next to our front door we keep a watercolor painting we found online. It is painted from the perspective of someone standing inside Bag End, the home of Bilbo and then Frodo Baggins in J. R. R. Tolkien's *The Hobbit* and *The Lord of the Rings*. It shows a stone road and rolling hills fading into a white-gold sky in the distance. The picture reminds us of the song Bilbo was so fond of singing, "The Road Goes Ever On and On."

It reminds us that the road runs right to our very door, and that road might take us anywhere and toward anything. It reminds us that there are no boring places in God's world—and no boring people, for that matter. It reminds us that God stands over and above his creation, calling us further up and further in. The road will lead to a cross. But only things that die can be resurrected. And so as sure as the road leads us to the cross, it leads us to the eternal city, to the home of the king, to the desire of all nations, to the joy of every longing heart.

ACKNOWLEDGMENTS

MY FRIEND GRAY SAID ONCE that Christians do not take enough time to speak kindly of their friends. He said it when I was a junior in college, but I've never forgotten it. So when I realized this book was actually going to happen, one of the first things I thought about was this section, my "giving of thanks," as Wendell Berry's character Hannah Coulter puts it at one point in the novel bearing her name. Here is mine.

Thank you to Bart Moseman, my first Reformed University Fellowship campus minister, pastor at CityLife Church, and now, best of all, my brother-in-law. Thank you also to Mike Hsu, pastor at Grace Vancouver Church and former pastor of Grace Chapel in Lincoln, the pastor who baptized me and received me into the membership of the church. Both of you received me into your communities during a vulnerable time in my life, and you loved me in all my anger, impatience, and suspicion. My debt to both of you—and your families!—is large. Thank you.

Thank you to Larry and Nancy Snyder and to Jock and Alison McGregor as well as Jo Ellen Park. During my time at Rochester L'Abri the five of you showed me that Christianity could be beautiful.

Thank you to Denis and Margie Haack and Anita Gorder. You showed Joie and me what home could be.

Thank you to Rod Dreher. Your generosity and enthusiasm is a large part of why this book happened at all.

Thank you to Philip, Missy, Evan, Anabelle, and Brooks Jensen for sharing work, food, and land with our family.

Thank you to James, Heidi, Sophie, Maria, Peter, and William Roland. Littlefield Abbey made the sabbath real to us.

Thank you to Eric Tonjes, KJ Drake, Matt Brittingham, John Roy, Tim Fangmeier, Gray Ewing, Jason Schafer, Craig Gant, Eric Cornell, and Micah Smith. Thank you for being friends who stick closer than a brother.

Thank you to Matt Anderson for answering an email from a confused college kid back in 2009, for asking me to write about Kony 2012, and for handing me the keys to *Mere Orthodoxy*.

Thank you to Brad Littlejohn for inviting me into the work of the Davenant Institute. Thank you to Steven Wedgeworth, Peter Escalante, Ben Miller, Susannah Black, Ian Clary, Scott Pryor, Mark Jones, Jordan Ballor, Brian Auten, Mark Olivero, and Rick Littlejohn for their fellowship on the Davenant Institute board.

Thank you to Derek Rishmawy, Jon Coppage, Matthew Loftus, Gracy Olmstead, Jon Askonas, Samuel James, and Chris Krycho for your friendship and support as I wrote this book.

Thank you to Peter Blair, Bria Sandford, Brandon McGinley, Charlie and Sarah Clark, Justin Hawkins, and Jose and Addie Mena for the gift of friendship and shared work with *Fare Forward*. Thanks especially to Charlie and Sarah for giving us the use of their home for a few days, where I was able to finish the manuscript.

Thank you to Stu Kerns and Keith Ghormley, pastors at Zion Church, for their friendship and trust. Thanks also to Gary Young for caring enough to regularly ask "How's the book coming?" Small kindnesses can mean a great deal.

Thank you to Ben Loos, pastor at Grace Chapel, for modeling imagination in preaching as well as an attentiveness to and reverence for the written word.

Thank you to my editor, Ethan McCarthy, and my agent, Don Gates, for making this book happen.

Thank you to Rob and Ruth Meador. "Let us all hope that we are preceded in this life by a love story." Thank you for guaranteeing that this would be true for me. You modeled faith in courageous, ordinary, and humble ways every day. My debt to you can never be repaid.

Finally, thank you to my daughter, Davy Joy, my sons, Wendell and Austin, and most of all to my wife, Joie. You sacrificed more than anyone else to make this book possible and you sustained my work on it with your love, encouragement, and presence. I pray that our home together would be a place where the things I have attempted to grasp in these pages would take on flesh.

NOTES

INTRODUCTION

[1]Steven Garber, *Visions of Vocation* (Downers Grove, IL: InterVarsity Press, 2014), 22.
[2]Michael Bible, "Is the US Facing an Epidemic of 'Deaths of Despair'? These Researchers Say Yes," *The Guardian*, March 28, 2017, www.theguardian.com /us-news/2017/mar/28/deaths-of-despair-us-jobs-drugs-alcohol-suicide.
[3]Oliver O'Donovan, *Common Objects of Love* (Grand Rapids: Eerdmans, 2002).
[4]Eric Tonjes, "Lie with Me Lover," 2018.
[5]Dante Alighiere, *Paradiso*, 1320, https://digitaldante.columbia.edu/dante /divine-comedy/paradiso/paradiso-33.

1 THE PASSING OF THE AMERICAN CHURCH

[1]Mark Driscoll, "There Is a Pile of Dead Bodies Behind the Mars Hill Bus," YouTube, November 3, 2012, www.youtube.com/watch?v=BfTmgPhmlto.
[2]Walter Brueggemann, *The Land* (Minneapolis: Augsburg Fortress, 2002), 4.
[3]Jay Michaelson, "Who Would Jesus Torture?" *Daily Beast*, January 18, 2015, www .thedailybeast.com/who-would-jesus-torture.
[4]Tara Isabella Burton, "Poll: White Evangelical Support for Trump is at an All-Time High," *Vox*, April 20, 2018, www.vox.com/identities/2018/4/20/17261726 /poll-prri-white-evangelical-support-for-trump-is-at-an-all-time-high.
[5]"Very Few Americans See Contraception as Morally Wrong," Pew Research Center, September 28, 2016, www.pewforum.org/2016/09/28/4-very-few-americans -see-contraception-as-morally-wrong.
[6]"Religious Belief and Views of Homosexuality," Pew Research Center, June 6, 2013, www.people-press.org/2013/06/06/section-3-religious-belief-and-views -of-homosexuality.
[7]"Survey Explores Who Qualifies as an Evangelical," Barna Research Group, January 18, 2007, www.barna.com/research/survey-explores-who-qualifies-as-an-evangelical.
[8]Emmanuel Katongole, *The Sacrifice of Africa* (Grand Rapids: Eerdmans, 2011), 2.
[9]See, for example, "Unam Sanctam" in which the fourteenth-century pope Boniface VIII clearly says that political powers must be subservient to spiritual powers. This is a clear papal teaching which cannot be changed, per the teachings of the Roman Catholic Church.

[10]The irony is that both of these moves are roughly mirror images of the move that mainline Protestants made with the urban bourgeois and progressive Americans decades prior.

[11]Paul F. M. Zahl, "Dust Became Mercy: A Word About My Friend Tullian," Tullian (blog), accessed May 13, 2018, www.tullian.net/articles/dust-became-mercy-a-word -about-my-friend-tullian.

[12]Oscar Romero, *The Scandal of Redemption* (Walden, NY: Plough Publishing, 2018), 83-84.

[13]C. Christopher Smith, "Not Your Father's Christian Community Development," *Christianity Today*, February 20, 2013, www.christianitytoday.com/thisisourcity /7thcity/not-your-fathers-christian-community-development.html?.

[14]Francis Schaeffer, *How Should We Then Live?* (Wheaton, IL: Crossway, 2005), 205.

[15]Emmanuel Katongole and Chris Rice, *Reconciling All Things* (Downers Grove, IL: InterVarsity Press, 2008), 43.

[16]Katongole and Rice, *Reconciling All Things*, 46.

[17]Romero, *Scandal of Redemption*, 131.

2 THE UNWINDING OF COMMON LIFE IN AMERICA

[1]John Paul II, "Evangelium Vitae," 22, Vatican, accessed July 11, 2018, https:// w2.vatican.va/content/john-paul-ii/en/encyclicals/documents/hf_jp-ii _enc_25031995_evangelium-vitae.html.

[2]Robert Putnam, *Bowling Alone* (New York: Simon & Schuster, 2000), 19.

[3]Henry Fountain, "The Lonely American Just Got a Bit Lonelier," *New York Times*, July 2, 2006.

[4]"New Cigna Study Reveals Loneliness at Epidemic Levels in America," Cigna, May 1, 2018, www.multivu.com/players/English/8294451-cigna-us-loneliness-survey.

[5]Jayne O'Donnell and Shari Rudavsky, "Young Americans Are the Loneliest, Surprising Study from Cigna Shows," *USA Today*, May 1, 2018, www.usatoday .com/story/news/politics/2018/05/01/loneliness-poor-health-reported-far -more-among-young-people-than-even-those-over-72/559961002.

[6]"Many Americans Are Lonely, and Gen Z Most of All, Study Finds," CBS News, May 3, 2018, www.cbsnews.com/news/many-americans-are-lonely-and-gen-z-most -of-all-study-finds.

[7]Mark Zuckerberg, Facebook, January 11, 2018, www.facebook.com/zuck /posts/10104413015393571.

[8]Katherine Hobson, "Feeling Lonely? Too Much Time on Social Media May Be Why," NPR, March 6, 2017, www.npr.org/sections/health-shots/2017 /03/06/518362255/feeling-lonely-too-much-time-on-social-media-may-be-why.

[9]Jean Twenge, "Have Smartphones Destroyed a Generation?" *The Atlantic*, September 2017.

[10]Benoit Denizet-Lewis, "Why Are More American Teenagers Than Ever Suffering from Severe Anxiety?" *New York Times*, October 11, 2017.

[11]Megan Garber, "Saving the Lost Art of Conversation," *Atlantic*, January-February 2014, www.theatlantic.com/magazine/archive/2014/01/the-eavesdropper/355727.

[12]Alex Morris, "Tales from the Millennial Sexual Revolution," *Rolling Stone,* March 31, 2014.

[13]Eleanor Barkhorn, "Getting Married Later Is Great for College-Educated Women," *Atlantic*, March 15, 2013, www.theatlantic.com/sexes/archive/2013/03 /getting-married-later-is-great-for-college-educated-women/274040.

[14]Julia Belluz, "The Historically Low Birthrate, Explained in Three Charts," *Vox*, May 22, 2018, www.vox.com/science-and-health/2018/5/22/17376536/fertility -rate-united-states-births-women.

[15]Charles Murray, *Coming Apart* (New York: Crown Forum, 2012), 158.

[16]Bruce Thornton, "The Coming Demographic Crisis: What to Expect When No One Is Expecting," Real Clear Politics, April 25, 2013, www.realclearpolitics .com/articles/2013/04/25/the_coming_demographic_crisis_what_to_expect _when_no_one_is_expecting_118128.html.

[17]"Be More Us," YouTube, May 9, 2018, www.youtube.com/watch?v=Pm 12mTIUJss.

[18]Hans Fiene, "Some Wise Words About Kids in Church," *A Lutheran Layman* (blog), accessed June 6, 2018, www.lutheranlayman.com/2018/05/some-wise -words-about-kids-in-church.html.

[19]Charlie Clark, "Book Review: The Children of Men by P. D. James," *Mere Orthodoxy*, May 11, 2017, https://mereorthodoxy.com/children-of-men-pd-james.

[20]Ronald Dworkin, "The Rise of the Caring Industry," Hoover Institution, June 2010.

[21]Stephen Marche, "Is Facebook Making Us Lonely?" *Atlantic*, May 2012, www.the atlantic.com/magazine/archive/2012/05/is-facebook-making-us-lonely/308930.

[22]Josh Katz, "You Draw It: Just How Bad Is the Drug Overdose Epidemic?" *New York Times,* October 26, 2017, www.nytimes.com/interactive/2017/04/14 /upshot/drug-overdose-epidemic-you-draw-it.html?_r=0.

[23]"Suicide Statistics," American Foundation for Suicide Prevention, accessed January 6, 2018, https://afsp.org/about-suicide/suicide-statistics.

[24]Eric Eyre, "Drug Firms Poured 780m Painkillers into WV Amid Rise of Overdoses," *Charleston Gazette-Mail*, December 17, 2016, www.wvgazettemail.com /news-health/20161217/drug-firms-poured-780m-painkillers-into-wv-amid -rise-of-overdoses.

[25]Katz, "You Draw It."

3 THE LOSS OF MEANING

[1]Stanley Hauerwas, "A Story-Formed Community: Reflections on *Watership Down*," *The Hauerwas Reader* (Durham, NC: Duke University Press, 2001), 172.

[2]Planned Parenthood v. Casey, 91-744, June 29, 1992, https://scholar.google.com /scholar_case?case=6298856056242550994&q=planned+parenthood+of+pennsylv ania+v.+casey&hl=en&as_sdt=6,33&as_vis=1#p851, accessed May 1, 2017.

[3]John Locke, *Second Treatise on Civil Government*, 1689, Constitution Society, accessed June 1, 2018, www.constitution.org/jl/2ndtr05.htm.

[4]Thomas Jefferson, quoted in Joseph Ellis, *American Sphinx* (New York: Random House, 1998), 131.

[5]Stanley Hauerwas, lecture at University of Nebraska-Lincoln, November 13, 2012.

[6]Jean-Paul Sartre, "Existentialism Is a Humanism," *Existentialism from Dostoyevsky to Sartre*, ed. Walter Kaufman (New York: Meridian, 1989), www.marxists.org /reference/archive/sartre/works/exist/sartre.htm.

[7]Simone de Beauvoir, *The Second Sex* (New York: Knopf, 1953), 301.

[8]de Beauvoir, *Second Sex*, 73.

[9]Albert Camus, *The Plague* (New York: Vintage Books, 1991), 308.

[10]Albert Camus, "The Myth of Sisyphus," University of Hawaii, accessed July 12, 2018, www2.hawaii.edu/~freeman/courses/phil360/16.%20Myth%20of%20 Sisyphus.pdf, 24.

[11]Stephen Schlesinger, "Trump and the Myth of Sisyphus," *Huffington Post*, updated November 16, 2017, www.huffingtonpost.com/stephen-schlesinger/trump -and-the-myth-of-sis_b_12994914.html.

[12]*Mad Men*, "The Wheel," season 1, episode 13, directed by Matthew Weiner, aired October 18, 2007, AMC.

[13]*This Is Us,* "Pilgrim Rick," season 1, episode 8, directed by Sarah Pia Anderson, aired November 22, 2016, NBC.

[14]Patrick Carr and Maria Kefalas, *Hollowing Out the Middle* (New York: Beacon Press, 2009).

[15]Timothy Keller, *Making Sense of God* (New York: Viking Penguin, 2016), 97.

[16]Ian Johnson, "Who Killed More: Hitler, Stalin, or Mao?," *New York Review of Books*, accessed July 19, 2018, www.nybooks.com/daily/2018/02/05/who-killed-more -hitler-stalin-or-mao.

[17]Marshall Berman, *The Politics of Authenticity* (New York: Verso, 2009), 24.

[18]Berman, *Politics of Authenticity*, 35.

[19]John Piper, *Desiring God* (Colorado Springs: Multnomah, 1986), 93.

[20]Alan Jacobs, *The Year of Our Lord 1943* (New York: Oxford University Press, 2018), 70.

[21]Paul VI, "Humanae Vitae," Vatican, 9, accessed July 16, 2018, http://w2 .vatican.va/content/paul-vi/en/encyclicals/documents/hf_p-vi_enc_25071968 _humanae-vitae.html.

[22]*Secondhand Lions,* directed by Tim McCanlies (Los Angeles: New Line Cinema, 2003).

[23]Dietrich Bonhoeffer, *Creation and Fall, Temptation* (New York: Macmillan, 1966), 37.

[24]Matthew Dickerson and David O'Hara, *Narnia and the Fields of Arbol* (Lexington: University of Kentucky Press, 2009), 127.

4 THE LOSS OF WONDER

[1]John Newton, quoted in John Piper, "John Newton: The Tough Roots of His Habitual Tenderness," *Desiring God* (blog), January 30, 2001, www.desiringgod .org/messages/john-newton-the-tough-roots-of-his-habitual-tenderness.

[2]Italo Calvino, *Invisible Cities, Ruan Yifeng* (blog), accessed July 27, 2018, www .ruanyifeng.com/calvino/2006/12/cities_three.html.

[3]Jon Bois, "17776," *SBNation,* accessed July 6, 2018, www.sbnation.com/a/17776 -football/intermission-part-3.

[4]T. S. Eliot, "Little Gidding," *Four Quartets* (Orlando: Harcourt Brace, 1971), 59.

[5]*Mad Men,* "Commissions and Fees," season 5, episode 12, directed by Christopher Manley, aired June 3, 2012, AMC.

[6]John Keats, "Ode to a Nightingale," 1819.

[7]Josh Ritter, "Girl in the War," *The Animal Years,* V2 Records, 2006.

[8]Franz Kafka, "A Message from the Emperor," 1919, *New York Review of Books,* accessed July 8, 2018, www.nybooks.com/daily/2011/07/01/message-emperor -new-translation.

[9]Joshua Rothman, "Rod Dreher's Monastic Vision," *New Yorker,* May 1, 2017.

[10]Neil deGraase Tyson (@neiltyson), "On this day long ago, a child was born who, by age 30, would transform the world. Happy Birthday Isaac Newton b. Dec 25, 1642," Twitter, December 5, 2014, 7:38 a.m., https://twitter.com/neiltyson/status /548140622826459136?lang=en.

[11]Matthew Schofield, "Romanian Villagers Decry Police Investigation Into Vampire Slaying," *McClatchy,* updated July 7, 2010, www.mcclatchydc.com/news /nation-world/world/article24587203.html.

[12]Steven Roberts, "White House Confirms Reagans Followed Astrology, Up to a Point," *New York Times,* May 4, 1988.

[13]Lucia Peters, "What Is 'Dear David'? Here Is Everything Writer Adam Ellis Has Tweeted About His Apartment, from Start to Finish," *Bustle,* January 12, 2018, www.bustle.com/p/what-is-dear-david-here-is-everything-writer-adam-ellis -has-tweeted-about-his-haunted-apartment-from-start-to-finish-7714979.

[14]David W. Moore, "Three in Four Americans Believe in Paranormal," *Gallup News Service,* accessed August 6, 2018, http://news.gallup.com/poll/16915/three-four -americans-believe-paranormal.aspx.

[15]Michael Lipka, "18% of Americans Say They've Seen a Ghost," Pew Research Center, October 30, 2015, www.pewresearch.org/fact-tank/2015/10/30/18-of -americans-say-theyve-seen-a-ghost.

[16]Max Kutner, "The Number of People on Food Stamps Is Falling. Here's Why," *Newsweek*, July 27, 2017, www.newsweek.com/people-food-stamps-snap -decline-participation-640500; Abigail Geiger and Gretchen Livingstone, "8 Facts About Love and Marriage in America," Pew Research Center, February 13, 2018, www.pewresearch.org/fact-tank/2017/02/13/5-facts-about-love-and-marriage.

[17]Charles Taylor, "Buffered and Porous Selves," *Immanent Frame*, September 2, 2008, http://blogs.ssrc.org/tif/2008/09/02/buffered-and-porous-selves.

[18]James K. A. Smith, *How (Not) to Be Secular* (Grand Rapids: Eerdmans, 2014).

[19]Alissa Wilkinson and Robert Joustra, *How to Survive the Apocalypse* (Grand Rapids: Eerdmans, 2016), 15.

[20]Alan Jacobs, "Fantasy and the Buffered Self," *New Atlantis*, winter 2014, www .thenewatlantis.com/publications/fantasy-and-the-buffered-self.

[21]Richard Winter, *Still Bored in a Culture of Entertainment* (Downers Grove, IL: InterVarsity Press, 2002), 65-66.

[22]Blaise Pascal, quoted in Winter, *Still Bored*, 16.

[23]Logan Pearsall Smith, quoted in Winter, *Still Bored*, 17.

[24]Walker Percy, *Lost in the Cosmos* (New York: Picador, 1983), 70-71.

[25]Percy, *Lost in the Cosmos*, 73.

[26]Smith, *How (Not) to Be Secular*, 64.

5 THE LOSS OF GOOD WORK

[1]Kevin O'Leary, "Kevin O'Leary Gets Honest About the Personal Sacrifices Successful People Must Make," *YouTube*, December 2017, www.youtube.com /watch?v=0yw7HSPsXWE&t=190s.

[2]Leah Libresco, "The Sad Secular Monks," *First Things*, August 28, 2012, www .firstthings.com/web-exclusives/2012/08/the-sad-secular-monks.

[3]"Gallup Daily: U.S. Employee Engagement," Gallup.com, accessed October 19, 2018, https://news.gallup.com/poll/180404/gallup-daily-employee-engagement .aspx.

[4]"State of the American Workplace," Gallup.com, accessed October 19, 2018, https://news.gallup.com/reports/199961/7.aspx?utm_source=SOAW&utm _campaign=StateofAmericanWorkplace&utm_medium=2013SOAWreport.

[5]"The Engaged Workplace," Gallup.com, accessed October 19, 2018, www .gallup.com/services/190118/engaged-workplace.aspx.

[6]"The Gallup Q12 Employee Engagement Questionnaire," Society for Human Resource Management, May 1, 2010, www.shrm.org/hr-today/news/hr-magazine /pages/0510fox3.aspx.

[7]Lauren Smiley, "The Shut-in Economy," *Matter*, March 25, 2015, https://medium .com/matter/the-shut-in-economy-ec3ec1294816.

[8]Jia Tolentino, "The Gig Economy Celebrates Working Yourself to Death," *New Yorker*, March 22, 2017, www.newyorker.com/culture/jia-tolentino/the-gig -economy-celebrates-working-yourself-to-death.

[9]Laura Dunn and Jef Sewell, dir., *Look and See: A Portrait of Wendell Berry* (United States: Two Birds Film, 2016).

[10]Nancy Pearcey, *Total Truth* (Wheaton, IL: Crossway Books, 2004), 329-30.

[11]C. R. Wiley, *Man of the House* (Eugene, OR: Wipf & Stock, 2017), 30.

[12]Wiley, *Man of the House*, 20.

[13]Bryan Miller, "Extreme Commuting," *New York Times*, July 21, 2017.

[14]Matthew Crawford, *Shop Class as Soul Craft* (New York: Penguin, 2010), 127-28.

[15]Drew DeSilver, "For Most Workers, Real Wages Have Barely Budged for Decades," Pew Research Center, August 7, 2018, www.pewresearch.org/fact-tank/2014/10/09 /for-most-workers-real-wages-have-barely-budged-for-decades.

[16]Jason DeParle, Robert Gebeloff, and Sabrina Tavernise, "Older, Suburban and Struggling, 'Near Poor' Startle the Census," *New York Times*, November 18, 2011, www.nytimes.com/2011/11/19/us/census-measures-those-not-quite-in-poverty-but -struggling.html?pagewanted=all.

[17]Richard J. Dougherty, "Catholicism and the Economy: Augustine and Aquinas on Property Ownership," *Journal of Markets & Morality* 6, no. 2 (2003): 479-95.

[18]Thomas Aquinas, *Summa Theologia* I-II, Q. 105.2, reply to obj. 1, www .newadvent.org/summa/2105.htm.

[19]John Calvin, *Commentary on the Book of the Prophet Isaiah*, trans. William Pringle, www.ccel.org/ccel/calvin/calcom13.i.html.

[20]Matthew Tuingina, "Aquinas and Calvin Believed Property Rights Were Subject to the Rights of the Poor," *Christian in America* (blog), September 19, 2012, https:// matthewtuininga.wordpress.com/2012/09/19/aquinas-and-calvin-believed -property-rights-were-subject-to-the-rights-of-the-poor.

[21]Francis I, *Evangelii Gaudium*, article 189, Vatican.com, accessed June 1, 2018, http:// w2.vatican.va/content/francesco/en/apost_exhortations/documents/papa -francesco_esortazione-ap_20131124_evangelii-gaudium.html.

[22]Milton Friedman, *Capitalism and Freedom* (Chicago: University of Chicago Press, 1962), 15.

[23]William Cavanaugh, *Being Consumed: Economics and Christian Desire* (Grand Rapids: Eerdmans, 2016), 18.

PART THREE: THE PRACTICES OF COMMUNITY

[1]Wendell Berry, interview by Bill Moyers. *Moyers and Company*, October 4, 2013, https://billmoyers.com/episode/wendell-berry-poet-prophet/.

[2]Herman Bavinck, *The Christian Family* (Grand Rapids: Christian's Library Press, 2012), 63.

6 SABBATH AND THE CHIEF END OF MAN

[1]Frederic Morton, *Crosstown Sabbath* (New York: Grove Press, 1987), 3.

[2]Morton, *Crosstown Sabbath*, 36.

[3]Abraham Heschel, *The Sabbath* (New York: Farrar, Straus, and Giroux, 1951), 3.

[4]Oscar Romero, *The Scandal of Redemption* (Walden, NY: Plough, 2018), 83.

[5]Jose Mena, "Understanding the Times: A Panel on Christianity, Liberalism, and the Challenges of Our Day," panel discussion, Washington, DC, January 10, 2018.

7 THE MEMBERSHIP

[1]Donald Miller, *Searching for God Knows What* (Nashville: Thomas Nelson, 2004), 105.

[2]Alfred, Lord Tennyson, "In Memoriam, A.H.H.," 1849.

[3]Reid Hoffman, Ben Casnocha, and Chris Yeh, "Your Company Is Not a Family," *Harvard Business Review*, June 17, 2014, https://hbr.org/2014/06/your -company-is-not-a-family.

[4]Patty McCord, quoted in Steve Henn, "How the Architect of Netflix's Innovative Culture Lost Her Job to the System," NPR, September 3, 2015, www .npr.org/2015/09/03/437291792/how-the-architect-of-netflixs-innovative -culture-lost-her-job-to-the-system.

[5] Julian Quinones and Arijeta Lajka, "What Kind of Society Do You Want to live in?: Inside the Country Where Down Syndrome Is Disappearing," www.cbsnews .com/news/down-syndrome-iceland/.

[6]Ellen Barry and Martin Selsoe Sorensen, "In Denmark, Harsh New Laws for Immigrant 'Ghettos,'" *New York Times*, July 1, 2018, www.nytimes.com/2018/07/01 /world/europe/denmark-immigrant-ghettos.html.

[7]Samuel Osborne, "Horrific Phone Calls Reveal How Italian Coast Guard Let Dozens of Refugees Drown," *Independent*, May 8, 2017, www.independent .co.uk/news/world/europe/italian-navy-lets-refugees-drown-migrants-crisis -asylum-seekers-mediterranean-sea-a7724156.html.

[8]Wendell Berry, *Jayber Crow* (Washington, DC: Counterpoint, 2000), 182.

[9]A. G. Sertillanges, *The Intellectual Life* (Washington, DC: Catholic University of America Press, 1998), 238-39.

[10]Norman Wirzba, *Food and Faith* (New York: Cambridge University Press, 2011), 146.

[11]James Wright, "Two Hangovers" in *The Branch Will Not Break* (Middletown, CT: Wesleyan University Press, 1959), 36.

[12]John Calvin, *Institutes of the Christian Religion* 1.1.1, ed. John T. McNeill (Philadelphia: Westminster Press, 1960), 36.

[13]Thomas Aquinas, quoted in Josef Pieper, *Guide to Thomas Aquinas* (San Francisco: Ignatius Press, 1991), 48.

[14]Thomas Aquinas, *Summa Contra Gentiles*, bk 3, chap. 122.

[15]John Calvin, *Commentary on the First Book of Moses Called Genesis*, www.ccel .org/ccel/calvin/calcom01.i.html.

[16]Wendell Berry, *What Are People For?* (San Francisco: North Point Press, 1990), 180.

[17]Oliver O'Donovan, *Resurrection and Moral Order* (Grand Rapids: Eerdmans, 1994), 70.

[18]Jeremy McLellan, "Thread by @JerryMcLellan," *Thread Reader*, accessed October 22, 2018, https://threadreaderapp.com/thread/1023908001353265152.html?refreshed=yes.

[19]Henri Nouwen, *Adam* (Maryknoll, NY: Orbis, 2013), 72-73.

[20]Nouwen, *Adam*, 72-73.

8 WORK

[1]John Stott, "When I Feel Most Alive," *YouTube*, August 6, 2010, www.youtube .com/watch?v=MDPqw-LauaU.

[2]Rodney Scott, "Why the Best Southern Barbecue Takes Weeks to Make—Southern Foodways Alliance," *YouTube*, July 13, 2016, www.youtube.com/watch?v =39ii9LvnDoE&t=684s.

[3]Alan Jacobs, *The Year of Our Lord, 1943* (New York: Oxford University Press, 2018), 201.

[4]Oliver O'Donovan, *Begotten or Made* (New York: Oxford University Press, 1984), 2-3.

[5]John Calvin, *Commentary on the First Book of Moses Called Genesis*, www.ccel .org/ccel/calvin/calcom01.i.html.

[6]Edith Schaeffer, *Hidden Art of Homemaking* (Carol Stream, IL: Tyndale House Publishers, 1985), 129-30.

[7]Harrison Higgins, in "Furniture Fit for the Kingdom" by Nathan Clarke, *Christianity Today*, May 1, 2012, www.christianitytoday.com/thisisourcity/richmond /furniturefit.html.

[8]Sarah Perry, "A Bad Carver," *Ribbonfarm* (blog), November 3, 2016, www .ribbonfarm.com/2016/11/03/a-bad-carver.

[9]Greg Gilbert and Sebastian Traeger, *The Gospel at Work* (Grand Rapids: Zondervan, 2018), 16.

[10]David Graeber, "On Bullshit Jobs," *STRIKE!*, August 2013.

[11]Nathan Heller, "The Bullshit Job Boom," *New Yorker*, June 7, 2018.

[12]Wendell Berry, *The Hidden Wound* (San Francisco: North Point Press, 1989), 121-22.

[13]Berry, *Hidden Wound*, 122.

[14]Mario Savio, "Sit-in Address on the Steps of Sproul Hall," *American Rhetoric*, December 2, 1964, www.americanrhetoric.com/speeches/mariosaviosproulhallsitin.htm.

9 POLITICAL DOCTRINE AND CIVIL VIRTUE

[1]Ross Douthat, "The Party of Julia," *New York Times*, May 5, 2012, www.nytimes .com/2012/05/06/opinion/sunday/douthat-the-party-of-julia.html.

[2]David Corn, "Secret Video: Romney Tells Millionaire Donors What He Really Thinks of Obama Voters," *Mother Jones*, September 17, 2012, www.motherjones .com/politics/2012/09/secret-video-romney-private-fundraiser.

[3]Andrew Willard Jones, *Before Church and State* (Steubenville, OH: Emmaus Academic, 2017), 13.

[4]Tim Keller, *Generous Justice* (New York: Penguin Random House, 2012), 170.

[5]David Koyzis, *Political Visions and Illusions* (Downers Grove, IL: InterVarsity Press, 2003), 230.

[6]John Adams, "From John Adams to Massachusetts Militia, 11 October 1798," Founders Online, accessed November 18, 2018, https://founders.archives.gov /documents/Adams/99-02-02-3102.

[7]Andy Crouch, *Playing God* (Downers Grove, IL: InterVarsity Press, 2013), 245.

[8]John Calvin, *Commentary on a Harmony of the Evangelists, Matthew, Mark, and Luke*, trans. William Pringle, www.ccel.org/ccel/calvin/calcom31.i.html.

[9]Calvin, *Commentary on a Harmony of the Evangelists*.

[10]Brett Samuels, "Jerry Falwell Jr.: Conservatives and Christians Need to Stop Electing 'Nice Guys,'" *The Hill*, September 30, 2018, https://thehill.com/blogs /blog-briefing-room/409151-jerry-falwell-jr-conservatives-and-christians-need -to-stop-electing.

[11]Alissa Wilkinson, "Views and Worldviews," *Comment*, January 28, 2011.

[12]Joe Pug, "Hymn #101," *Joe Pug*, accessed November 18, 2018, http://joepugmusic .com/lyrics/hymn-101.

[13]Peter Escalante and Alistair Roberts, "Protestant Wisdom," Davenant Institute, accessed October 24, 2018, https://davenantinstitute.org/summer-programs-ca.

10 THE ETERNAL CITY

[1]Al Wolters, *Creation Regained* (Grand Rapids: Eerdmans, 2005), 69.

[2]Wolters, *Creation Regained*, 47-48.

[3]Robert Farrar Capon, *The Supper of the Lamb* (New York: Farrar, Straus & Giroux, 1989), 180.

[4]C. S. Lewis, *The Last Battle* (New York: Harper Collins, 1984), 224.

"Indebted to his own deep Nebraskan roots (and to thoughtful others far beyond his local community), Meador has written a clear, compelling, and distinctly Christian volume focused on restoring communal flourishing."

Mark P. Ryan, Covenant Theological Seminary, St. Louis, director of the Francis A. Schaeffer Institute

"Meador's book somehow manages to pair a trenchant diagnosis of our polarized communities with a hopeful prognosis built on a deep theological conception of the good life. It challenges but does not provoke. It offers hope without presumption. . . . This is exactly why this book deserves to find a wide readership."

David Henreckson, Dordt College

"Drawing on the wisdom of Scripture, natural law, and the practices of the Christian tradition, Jake points us to a vision of work, community, and politics attuned to the rhythms of creation, reflective of the eternal city, and ultimately rooted in the goodness of God himself."

Derek Rishmawy, columnist at *Christianity Today*, cohost of *Mere Fidelity* podcast

"I've long admired the breadth of knowledge on display in Jake Meador's writing. You'll see his characteristic combination of deep learning with an earthy touch in this wide-ranging book. You won't need to agree with every conclusion in order to appreciate how he makes you think and act more deliberately."

Collin Hansen, editorial director for The Gospel Coalition

"Jake's book accurately diagnoses some of the ills of our modern world and, even more importantly, provides a vivid, specific vision of a full and flourishing Christian life."

Leah Libresco, author of *Building the Benedict Option* and *Arriving at Amen*

"Jake Meador is one of the most insightful evangelical writers of his generation. Without downplaying the severity of the crises that are currently crippling both our churches and our country, he nevertheless sketches what a quietly hopeful Christian witness in our troubled times might look like. By turns diagnostic, instructive, expository, and artful and with a disarming lack of cynicism throughout, this moving book channels Wendell Berry in arguing for the renewable dignity of disappearing virtues."

Wesley Hill, associate professor of biblical studies, Trinity School for Ministry, Ambridge, Pennsylvania

"What if the malaise that grips American communities is the fruit of a church that has failed to bear faithful witness to her King? Jake Meador's convicting yet hope-giving book calls the church to take up the practice of distinctively Christian forms of membership in order to serve the common good. Meador reminds us that when Christians pursue hidden fidelity rather than public praise, sacrificial service rather than personal peace and affluence, and patient catechesis rather than flashy policy proposals, it is then that they will bless their neighbors."

Jeffrey Bilbro, author of *Virtues of Renewal: Wendell Berry's Sustainable Forms*, editor in chief at Front Porch Republic

"If the bonds of modern society show signs of strain, it is in part because the goods we share as members have ceased to be common or perceived as good. Yet, as Jake Meador reminds us in *In Search of the Common Good*, the love that unites us around the goods we share in common is reaffirmed through our practices of community and renewed by the promise of community. Meador has provided here an important recovery of the deeply Christian notion of the common good, offering a knowledgeable diagnosis of the common good's fall into disfavor and an equally knowledgeable proposal for recovering it. Meador reminds us that the common good is worth searching for, and in searching for it we share in it together, eager for all to receive the gifts God has given. Read this book—for you and for your community."
Matthew Arbo, assistant professor of theological studies, director of the Center for Faith and Public Life

"*In Search of the Common Good* is not just a good book, it is a necessary book for our time. Jake diagnoses many of the deep problems in our society and offers a distinctly Christian path forward. I have already begun recommending the book widely, and I suspect that the church in America will be reading and discussing it for a long time to come."
Alan Noble, author of *Disruptive Witness*

"In this beautiful and compelling book, Meador offers readers more than a list of our societal ills. He offers us hope—and a clear and steady path to restoring our homes, churches, and communities. For those already on that path, *In Search of the Common Good* will breathe new life into their efforts, encouraging them that their lives of quiet faithfulness and goodness are far more significant than they realize. And for those still finding their way, Meador's words beckon us to the path of life."
Hannah Anderson, author of *Humble Roots* and *All That's Good*

"*In Search of the Common Good* offers a vision for life together that is deep, compelling, and wise. This is a profound and important work by an exceptional writer."
Karen Swallow Prior, author of *On Reading Well* and *Fierce Convictions*

"*In Search of the Common Good* is for Christians with hungry souls—Christians seeking more than our stressed and fractured culture can provide. Meador's work pushes us beyond the realm of political vitriol and atomistic individualism toward real flourishing. He prompts us to consider the world beyond our heads, the entire fabric of creation and community that we have so long neglected—and thus proffers an essential vision for Christians living in our society. This book is ecumenical and inspiring, but most of all, it is right."
Gracy Olmstead, The American Conservative

"Jake Meador has written a learned cri de coeur that situates the division and confusion American Christians face, not in politics, but in our theological imaginations. Carefully analyzing the sources of anger and despair in American life through the lens of the ideas about the common good advanced by Christian luminaries from the church fathers to the Reformers, Meador shows how a renewed understanding of the common good leads out of despair toward hope."
Jonathan D. Askonas, assistant professor of politics at the Catholic University of America, fellow at the Center for the Study of Statesmanship